HOW TO GROW YOUR OWN FOOD

An Illustrated Beginner's Guide to Container Gardening

ANGELA S. JUDD

ADAMS MEDIA
New York London Toronto Sydney New Delhi

Aadamsmedia

Adams Media
An Imprint of Simon & Schuster, Inc.
100 Technology Center Drive
Stoughton, Massachusetts 02072

Copyright © 2021 by Simon & Schuster, Inc.

First Adams Media hardcover edition May 2021

ADAMS MEDIA and colophon are trademarks of Simon & Schuster.

For information about special discounts for bulk purchases, please contact Simon & Schuster Special Sales at 1-866-506-1949 or business@ simonandschuster.com.

The Simon & Schuster Speakers Bureau can bring authors to your live event. For more information or to book an event contact the Simon & Schuster Speakers Bureau at 1-866-248-3049 or visit our website at www.simonspeakers.com.

Interior design by Priscilla Yuen
Illustrations by Nicola DosSantos
Interior images © 123RF/Algirdas Urbonavicius, Anna Kutukova, roystudio

Manufactured in China

10 9 8 7 6 5 4

Library of Congress Cataloging-in-Publication Data has been applied for.

ISBN 978-1-5072-1572-2
ISBN 978-1-5072-1573-9 (ebook)

For Haley (my favorite millennial),
who wants to garden but isn't sure where to begin.

———————————

Thanks to my husband, Jeff, without whose patience in editing and parenting, combined with his love, encouragement, and late-night pep talks, this book would not have happened. To our children, Haley, Dallin, Grant, Tyler, and Calvin, who encouraged me and kept the chaos to a minimum while I was writing. A special shout-out to Tyler, who gave up his bedroom so I could have an office while everyone was home during the pandemic.

Love and appreciation to my mom, who kept my family well fed while I was busy writing. Also, thanks to Julia Jacques, editor at Adams Media, for giving me the opportunity to write this book.

Finally, I'm grateful to everyone who has nurtured my green thumb and taught me to see the magic inside a seed and the joy of spending time in a garden.

———————————

Contents

CHAPTER 4

Helpful Terms to Know

CHAPTER 5

Vegetables, Herbs, Fruits, and Edible Flowers

Appendix A: Troubleshooting Advice and a Quick Reference Guide for Organic Pest Control 134

Appendix B: Resources to Learn More about Container Gardening 138

Introduction

Are you looking to grow your own organic food but feel like you don't have the skills or knowledge to do it?

Maybe you only have a limited amount of outdoor space...or possibly even none! Perhaps you've only experimented with growing house plants, and the idea of growing actual fruits and vegetables seems a bit more complicated. Maybe you're excited to get growing...but simply wondering where to start.

No matter where you are, *How to Grow Your Own Food* will give you the knowledge and confidence to successfully grow your own food in containers. Container gardening is a simple way to begin gardening and ideal if you have limited experience and/or space. If you have a balcony, patio, patch of grass, or even a driveway or sidewalk, you can add a container or two and get started right away! Container gardening is also a great option if you have a garden but would like to add more space, lengthen your growing seasons, or grow some plants indoors.

In this book you'll learn about:

- The "why" of gardening—the basic principles of gardening that will help you successfully grow your own food.
- The "what" of gardening—what exactly you need to get started growing your own food.
- The "how" of gardening—how to grow your own food in containers (including easy-to-understand steps that take you through planning, setting up, planting, and caring for your container garden).

You'll also find a list of fifty plants that grow well in containers, all with illustrations, in-depth growing instructions, and tips. Find a vegetable, herb, flower, or fruit that catches your eye, then read about how to grow it. Find the right container for the selected plants, and you are ready to begin planting! Build on your successes and learn from your mistakes each season. And don't forget to add more containers as your experience and confidence grow...along with your garden!

How to Use This Book

Are you ready to grow your own food? In Chapter 5, you'll find listings for dozens of plants to get you started. If you're a beginner, consider paying special attention to the ones that are easiest to grow. Under the "Difficulty" section for each plant, three levels are listed:

LEVEL 1: EASY
These plants are simple to grow and have the fewest steps from planting to harvest.

LEVEL 2: MEDIUM
These plants may have a couple of extra steps required for growing success—and there are things to look out for along the way.

LEVEL 3: DIFFICULT
These plants can be difficult to grow for various reasons—but don't be afraid to give them a try! Level 3 crops require more effort, but everything you need to know is included in the entry. Read the growing information carefully and follow each step to be successful.

Choosing the right container for the plants you select is crucial. Each entry details the minimum size to use for that plant to thrive. Use the "Container Sizes" section in Chapter 2 to determine what size container your plant needs. When you select the right-size container, your new plant will have enough soil, air, water, and nutrients to happily grow and provide you with a delicious harvest.

Pay attention to the light requirements in each entry, and place your containers where they will receive enough sun. Follow the guidelines of the "When to Plant" sections for the greatest chance of a successful harvest. As questions arise, consult Chapter 4: Helpful Terms to Know, as well as the tables in Appendix A, which provide simple, clear information on troubleshooting common problems and information on how to manage pests in a safe, organic way.

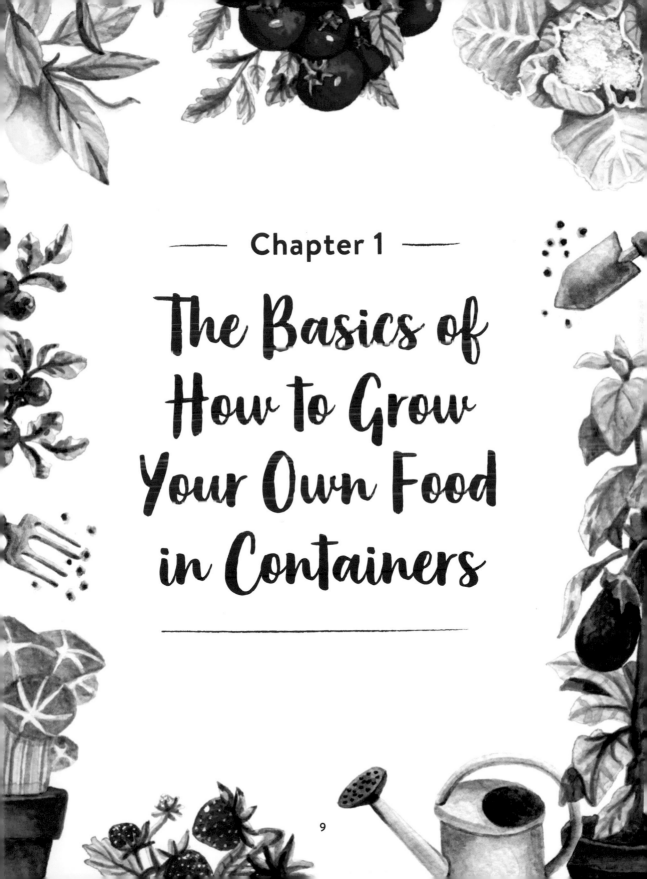

Chapter 1

The Basics of How to Grow Your Own Food in Containers

The idea of growing your own food may seem complicated, but in reality, learning to grow food in containers can be simple. Whether you are a beginning or advanced gardener, container gardening is a practical way to be more self-sufficient and aware of where your food comes from. You may already be using containers to grow plants such as houseplants or that pot of flowers by the front door. This chapter will teach you how to take some of the basic gardening skills you may already have, add to them, and then learn how to grow your own food in those same types of containers.

This chapter will also explain ten principles for successful container gardening. As you begin your container-gardening journey, make sure you understand each of these principles. As you progress, if you notice a problem with your garden, read through the gardening principles again. It's possible one of your plant's basic needs is not being met.

The Benefits of Growing Food in Containers

As you read through the benefits in this section, hopefully you'll come to realize that gardening doesn't need to be expensive or complicated. Growing food in containers simplifies the process of traditional gardening and removes some common obstacles to getting started.

YOU CAN GROW FOOD ANYWHERE

One of the biggest benefits of container gardening is the ability to do it anywhere. Add a container to a balcony, deck, or sidewalk, and you're ready to go. No room outdoors? With the proper light, you can even grow indoors.

YOU GROW FOOD IN THE BEST SOIL RIGHT AWAY

The soil in traditional in-bed gardens can take years to develop. Containers are filled with the best type of soil for vegetables, herbs, fruits, and flowers to grow in from the start, and issues with ground contamination, poor soil, rocky soil, weeds, or other issues are avoided. Soil-borne pests and diseases common to in-ground beds are often avoided or lessened by moving the plants out of the ground and into containers. In addition, pH (a measurement of the soil's acidity or alkalinity) is simpler to manage and adjust in containers by using different types of potting soil.

IT'S SIMPLE AND INEXPENSIVE TO GET STARTED

The startup costs and preparation associated with container gardening are minimal, especially if you start small. It is simple to get started (no need for preparing soil or buying a shovel, rake, or wheelbarrow), and you won't need a truckload of soil dropped off at your house in order to begin. The tools necessary for container gardening are minimal and explained in detail in Chapter 2.

CONTAINER GARDENS ARE ADAPTABLE AND ACCESSIBLE FOR ALMOST EVERYONE

An added benefit of containers over traditional in-ground beds is that they are adaptable and can be made accessible for most situations. For instance, a container's height can be adjusted by placing it on a railing, bench, or ledge. There is also less bending, digging, and kneeling required than with in-ground beds.

IT ALLOWS FOR FLEXIBILITY IN LOCATION AND TIMING

A container garden is portable. If your location needs to change, your garden can come along. You can move containers to the sunniest parts of your yard or take them indoors to escape extremes of heat or cold. Additionally, because containers are portable and heat up (and cool down) more quickly than in-ground gardens, they can extend the growing seasons of vegetables, herbs, fruits, and flowers.

Ten Principles for Successful Container Gardening

These basic principles will give you a straightforward understanding of the "why" behind gardening. As you learn and apply these principles, you will minimize and avoid problems but be equipped to troubleshoot them if they do occur in your garden.

PLANTS NEED ADEQUATE LIGHT TO PRODUCE FOOD

The most important principle for gardening success is sunlight. Although some plants need very little, plants grown for food need abundant light. Some vegetables will tolerate shade more than others, but all need sun. Most of the fruits, vegetables, herbs, and flowers discussed in this book do best with 6–8 hours of sunlight. For example:

- Flowering plants need a minimum of 6 hours of direct sunlight.
- Plants grown for the edible roots need a minimum of 4 hours of direct sunlight.
- Plants grown for the edible leaves need a minimum of 3 hours of direct sunlight.

If you are growing indoors, you will need a grow light. Plants that don't get enough sun grow slowly, if at all. If you have a choice between morning sun and afternoon sun, choose morning sun. A spot that gets 6–8 hours of sun beginning in the morning and then has a little afternoon shade is ideal for growing most fruits and vegetables.

PLANT AT THE IDEAL TIME AND TEMPERATURE FOR EACH PLANT

Every vegetable, herb, fruit, and flower has a preferred growing temperature. Planting at the correct time for each one is a key factor in the success of your harvest. Some crops prefer cooler weather and tolerate a little frost; others need warmer weather to grow well and would die in frosty conditions. A big part of gardening success is learning the unique growing conditions of your area. Plants are happiest and grow best when they are planted at the ideal soil temperature.

PLANTS IN CONTAINERS NEED DIFFERENT SOIL THAN PLANTS IN THE GROUND

Regular garden soil is too compact and heavy for container gardening and does not provide the air and water necessary for the roots to grow. The right mixture of ingredients in potting soil provides nutrients, air, and water for the roots, and it gives your plants the best chance of success. For more information about the preferred mixture for containers, see Chapter 2.

WATERING CORRECTLY IS CRUCIAL FOR CONTAINER GARDENING

Without adequate water, plants will die. Plants' roots in containers cannot search out water sources like their in-ground counterparts can. As the gardener, you are responsible for meeting your plants' watering needs. Plants are made mostly of water and use water for photosynthesis and transpiration. When your plant doesn't get enough water, the root hairs on the plant wither and can't take in nutrients any longer. Soil also needs water to live and to transfer energy to the plant. When the soil dries out, the living things in the soil go dormant or die and cannot feed your plant. Water brings life and growth to your plants—and makes delicious food possible.

PLANTS (AND THEIR ROOTS) NEED AIR TO GROW

Too much water can be as damaging to plants as too little. If the spaces between the soil particles are taken up with water, there is no room for air. Without air, the roots suffocate and die. You may have seen the hole in the bottom of a container and wondered if it is really necessary. The answer is yes! The hole allows excess water to drain out of the container. Likewise, lifting the container up off the ground with bricks or a plant caddy allows the water to drain freely out of the hole.

This principle applies above the soil as well. Adequate airflow around plants is necessary for healthy, happy plants. Crowding plants too close together or growing plants in areas with poor airflow causes problems with disease.

CONTAINER-GROWN PLANTS REQUIRE MORE FREQUENT FERTILIZATION

Because nutrients are leeched out of the drain hole of the container and plants in containers cannot seek out nutrients in surrounding soil, they rely on you to feed them. Quality potting soil has some nutrients, but most plants require additional fertilizer. The best way to feed plants is through regularly applying organic fertilizer.

PLANT ROOTS NEED ENOUGH ROOM TO GROW

Have you ever seen a picture of a large tree with a representation of its roots below ground? A tree's roots often extend the entire width of the tree's canopy and several feet below ground. This is a principle that applies to container gardening as well. Larger plants have larger root zones and need adequate-sized containers in order to grow a large enough root structure. The size of a plant is usually limited by the container in which it is grown. The size of your container should correlate to the size and number of plants grown in that container for the best chance of success.

CERTAIN VARIETIES OF PLANTS GROW WELL IN CONTAINERS

Because containers limit the size of the roots and available water, some plants are better suited to grow in containers. When choosing plants to grow in containers, look for "dwarf" varieties. These are smaller versions of full-size plants that do better in containers. Also, select "bush" varieties rather than vining types. "Compact" in the name is another clue that the variety will fare well in containers.

MANY CROPS IN CONTAINERS ARE HAPPIEST GROWN VERTICALLY

Growing vining plants vertically by adding a trellis to your container has many advantages. Vegetables grown vertically take up less space and have better airflow and exposure to sunlight, which gives them added resistance to pests and disease. It's also easier to harvest fruits and vegetables grown vertically. Plants left to spill out of containers onto the ground can be damaged by bugs or by getting stepped on.

THE BEST DEFENSE AGAINST PESTS AND DISEASE IS HEALTHY PLANTS

Healthy plants are less susceptible to disease and less attractive to pests. Do what you can to provide the optimal growing conditions, and plants will be healthier and have fewer problems. A major benefit of growing your own food is the knowledge of how that food was grown; don't give up on organic gardening and spray chemicals on every bug you see. Use the tables in Appendix A to help you troubleshoot issues while they are small. Always use the least invasive method first and be patient.

Chapter 2

Tools of the Trade and Guide to Containers

Most of what you'll need for container gardening will fit in a small bucket or basket. This chapter will provide you with a list of recommended supplies. You may even discover that you have some of them already on hand. The right tools will make your job easier. Purchase the best tools you can afford and take good care of them. Clean off dirt and debris after each use. Find a spot to store your supplies so you know where they are when you need them. Keeping your tools and supplies well organized helps maximize the time you have to spend in the garden.

The containers you choose are the most important "tools" you'll use. The size of container you need depends upon which plants you choose to grow. When you have a choice between a smaller or larger container, choose the larger container. A larger container means more soil, water, and air for your plants.

Tools of the Trade

You may not need all of the items listed here to get started. Begin by gathering a few basics and then add to your tools as the need arises.

GARDEN FABRIC Garden fabric serves many purposes, including pest control, protection for seedlings from birds, and shielding the plant from hot and cold weather. It is also called row cover or floating row cover.

GARDEN SCOOP Use a garden scoop to easily scoop soil out of bags and into your containers.

GLOVES Some gardeners never use gloves; others won't garden without them. You may want to use them for the biggest jobs at the beginning or end of the growing season.

HAND PRUNERS A little larger than pruning shears, hand pruners can harvest larger items like squash and are good for cutting through thicker branches and stems.

HAND TROWEL Think of this as your shovel for container gardening. With the trowel, you can dig down into the soil to dig a hole for your plants. Find one that feels comfortable in your hands.

HARVEST BASKET Think positive and find a basket you can't wait to fill with the bounty from your garden. While it's waiting for vegetables, you can store your garden tools inside it.

ORGANIC FERTILIZER Organic fertilizers provide both macronutrients and micronutrients and are less likely to burn plants than synthetic fertilizers. Good organic fertilizers for container gardening include liquid fish and seaweed fertilizers.

PLANT DOLLY If a pot is going to be moved indoors or to another location, put heavy containers on a plant dolly with wheels before filling it with dirt and plants.

PLANT LABELS Use plant labels to record what and when you plant.

PRUNING SHEARS/SNIPS Perfect for snipping herbs, deadheading flowers, and harvesting small vegetables. Their small size allows you to thin plants and snip as needed.

SOIL THERMOMETER Many of the entries in this book list a temperature guide for knowing when to plant. This handy tool takes some of the guesswork out of when to plant. For an accurate reading, take the temperature of the soil first thing in the morning and place the probe 2"–4" deep for a few minutes.

TRELLIS A trellis can be something like a tomato cage, bamboo poles sunk into the container, or a lattice attached to a nearby wall—any structure on which vining plants are encouraged to climb and grow upward. Use caution with tall trellises to ensure they are firmly attached to the container or nearby wall to avoid tipping over.

A Word on Potting Soil

Potting soil is a key ingredient to container gardening. Garden soil is too heavy for containers. The best type of soil for containers is potting mix with a combination of compost, coconut coir or peat moss, and vermiculite or perlite. Look for a bagged potting mix with these ingredients. The potting soil should be light, fluffy, and drain well. If you can't find a premixed potting soil, consider mixing your own. Use an equal amount of each of the following ingredients:

COCONUT COIR OR PEAT MOSS holds air and water and decays very slowly (coconut coir is considered a more sustainable option than peat moss).

COMPOST provides organic matter and nutrients and increases the water-holding capacity of soil.

VERMICULITE OR PERLITE holds air and water and keeps soil light and airy. Vermiculite also adds calcium, magnesium, and potassium.

For most plants, regular potting soil is the right pH. However, a few plants prefer more acidic soil (these preferences are noted in the plant descriptions in Chapter 5). For these plants, buy an acidic potting soil to put in your containers. The label on the bag of soil will indicate if it is intended for such plants.

Planting Date Information

As was discussed in the gardening principles section, planting at the correct time for each plant is fundamental to success in growing your own food. The following tools will help you determine the correct time based on your location.

LOCAL PLANTING GUIDE A reliable planting guide meant for your area is an invaluable tool when gardening. A good way to find one is by contacting your local county extension office. If no county extension office is available, ask at a locally owned nursery if they can recommend a planting guide.

LOCAL FROST DATES Learn the dates of your average last spring and first fall frost. To find your dates, go to www.almanac.com/gardening/frostdates.

The planting times in the plant descriptions in Chapter 5 often refer to these dates. The number of days between those dates are your "growing season." Colder areas have a shorter growing season than warmer areas. Understanding the length of your growing season allows you to select vegetable varieties well suited to your area.

LOCAL USDA GROWING ZONE For fruit trees and perennial plants, it is also important to know your USDA growing zone. To learn your zone, go to https://planthardiness.ars.usda.gov/PHZMWeb and enter your zip code. Awareness of your growing zone helps you know which fruit trees will survive outdoors or know if containers need to be brought inside during cold months.

Watering Concerns

Watering incorrectly is often the cause of many problems in the garden. The following tools make time spent watering more efficient and effective.

HOSE A garden hose makes watering easier. Plants in containers often need watering every day. Look for a hose that is long enough to reach your containers.

MOISTURE METER A moisture meter indicates when to water and helps prevent overwatering. The probe measures the moisture level at root level and displays it on the meter.

OLLAS An olla is an unglazed clay pot, normally with a wide bottom and narrow neck. The wider part of the vessel is buried below ground with the neck above ground. Fill the olla with water, and the water seeps out slowly through the porous clay. Ollas give water to the roots over a period of time. They are a good option for thirsty plants, hot climates, or if you go out of town frequently.

SELF-WATERING CONTAINERS These containers have a reservoir for water in the base of the container. A wick in the root area sucks up water from the reservoir. Water is added to fill the reservoir as needed. These containers usually don't need a hole at the bottom for drainage. Self-watering containers are another good option if you can't water your garden every day.

SPRAY NOZZLE The nozzle attaches to the end of the hose and usually adjusts to different patterns. Look for one with a shower option. The shower setting wets the soil evenly without disrupting it too much and exposing roots.

WATERING CAN Use a watering can to mix liquid fertilizers and water before adding them to your plants. Also, if proximity to a water spigot isn't possible, use a watering can to water the containers. This method is the most time-consuming way to water and only works best if you have a few small containers.

A Guide to Container Styles

Before getting into specifics, there is one important rule to note for any container you are considering for your plants: There must be a hole in the bottom to allow excess water to drain out so that roots and soil do not become waterlogged. Larger containers may have several holes to allow for more drainage.

Additionally, depending on what the container is placed on, you may need to lift up the container to improve airflow and drainage. Use pot feet, bricks, or small pieces of wood placed around the perimeter underneath the container to allow excess water to flow out freely.

CONTAINER MATERIAL TYPES

Containers appropriate for gardening come in several different materials. Here are some of the choices you may encounter.

FABRIC
PROS: Portable—fabric pots often have handles, which makes moving them easier; material allows plants to breathe; sides can be rolled down to allow sunlight in; inexpensive, easy to store when not in use.
CONS: Soil dries out quickly.

FIBERGLASS AND PLASTIC
PROS: Lightweight; inexpensive; waterproof; retains moisture.
CONS: Dark-colored containers can get hot and heat up roots.

GLAZED TERRA COTTA
PROS: Waterproof; retains moisture; insulates plants; regulates temperature.
CONS: Often expensive; breakable; may freeze or crack in cold climates; large sizes are heavy.

METAL

PROS: Durable; retains moisture.
CONS: Temperatures fluctuate more than in other containers; roots can heat up excessively; best not to use in full sun.

UNGLAZED TERRA COTTA

PROS: Allows roots to breathe; inexpensive; insulates plants; regulates temperature.

CONS: Soil dries out quickly; breakable; may freeze or crack in cold climates; large sizes are heavy.

WOOD

PROS: Breathable; cedar and redwood are resistant to rot; insulates plants; regulates temperature.
CONS: Some varieties can rot.

Container Sizes

For the purposes of this book, containers are divided into the following five categories: extra-small, small, medium, large, and extra-large.

Use the amount of soil the container holds as a guideline for the container size. Containers that hold less than the amounts listed are not recommended for growing most vegetables to maturity. Generally, aim for the container to be as deep as it is wide. This provides the most room for the roots. The minimum recommended container size for each plant is listed on the plant entry pages in Chapter 5 of this book. Choose the largest possible container for vegetables to give them access to more soil, food, and water. Smaller containers need to be watered more frequently as well, so larger container sizes mean less work for you!

For the record, pot sizes are not standardized and often use different types of measurements (liquid, dry, and so on). Following are general guidelines in dry-soil measurements.

EXTRA-SMALL Holds up to 2 gallons (.3 cubic feet) of soil. Examples include an 8½" terra cotta or nursery pot and a 10" hanging basket.

SMALL Holds up to 3 gallons (.46 cubic feet) of soil. Examples include 10" terra cotta or nursery pots and a 14" hanging basket.

MEDIUM Holds up to 5 gallons (.69 cubic feet) of soil. Examples include a 5-gallon plastic bucket, a 12" terra cotta or nursery pot, and a half-bushel basket.

LARGE Holds up to 10 gallons (1.5 cubic feet) of soil. Examples include 16" terra cotta or nursery pots, a 10-gallon fabric pot, and a 1-bushel basket.

EXTRA-LARGE Holds up to 20 gallons (2.73 cubic feet) or more of soil. Examples include 18" terra cotta pots (2.3 cubic feet of soil), 24" terra cotta pots (3.8 cubic feet of soil), and half wine barrels (4.3 cubic feet of soil).

Chapter 3

Ten Steps to Successfully Growing Your Own Food in Containers

Are you ready to get started? This chapter walks you through the steps of planning, setting up, planting, and caring for your container garden. Start small—a container or two is a great way to begin and gain experience. Fine-tune your system and learn what methods work best for you. Expand your garden as your ability grows.

1. Choose the Best Location for Your Container Garden

The most important consideration is how much sun the area receives. Pay attention to the spot at different times of day. Ideally, the location for your containers receives at least 6–8 hours of sun throughout the day. If you have a choice, pick an area that receives morning sun. Hopefully, there is easy access to water in this location as well.

2. Decide What You Are Going to Plant

Spend some time looking through the fifty different vegetables, herbs, fruits, and flowers in Chapter 5. Make a list of what you would like to grow. Wondering which ones to choose? Grow what you like to eat and maybe try something new as well. If the sunlight in your garden is limited (less than 6 hours), choose plants that can tolerate partial shade.

Within the list of plants you would like to grow, use your planting guide to find out which ones do well in your area and the best time to plant them. Pay attention to the adjectives in the plant descriptions: cold-loving, heat-loving, cold-season, warm-season, long-season, short-season. These are clues to help you know when to plant. The soil temperature guidelines in several plant descriptions are also a helpful aid in determining when to plant.

Now evaluate the space you have available. Make sure you have enough room to grow your selected crops. Read through the plant information carefully and then decide if you need seeds or transplants. Make a list of what you need. Head to your local nursery for seeds and/or transplants, or check the online resources in the back of this book to buy seeds.

If you are buying transplants, keep these things in mind:

- Bigger doesn't mean better. Choose transplants that are short and compact rather than stretched out and overgrown.

- Avoid transplants with roots growing out of the bottom of the container and vegetables that have already blossomed.

- Look for healthy green leaves; discolored leaves may be signs of pests or disease.

3. Choose and Prepare the Containers for Your Selected Plants

Look at the plant listings in this book and choose the correct-size containers for the vegetables you are going to plant. Then:

- Make sure the containers you are using have drainage holes (unless it is a self-watering container).
- Clean out containers (even new ones) using soapy water with a little bleach added, and rinse well.
- Allow the containers to dry overnight, if possible, to minimize disease and insect problems.

It's okay and often beneficial to grow different plants in the same container at the same time. Many vegetables and herbs grow better together. Good companions for most entries are listed in the plant descriptions. Different plants grown in the same container should have similar light and watering requirements. Choose a large enough container to allow sufficient room for each of the plants. Adequate airflow between plants is an important part of keeping plants healthy.

4. Fill Containers with Soil

Put your pots in place. Be sure to add pot feet or a plant dolly underneath if necessary. Don't add any filler (rocks, packing peanuts, and so on) to the bottom of the container. The more soil, nutrients, and water available for your plants, the better! Once your containers are in place, fill them with soil. For a large container, you may want to fill it halfway and then spray it down with water before adding the rest of the soil so that the soil begins absorbing moisture. Fill the container to within an inch or two of the top. Once the container is full, use a hose with a shower attachment to thoroughly moisten it.

5. Plant Seeds and Transplants Correctly in Your Containers

Space and plant seeds according to the directions on the seed package and in the plant guidelines. Before planting transplants, water them well. Then, using your trowel, dig a hole for your plant and place the transplant in your container at the same level it was in the nursery pot (unless otherwise instructed in the planting directions). Water seeds and transplants thoroughly, being careful not to displace seeds or expose roots.

6. Water Your Garden Correctly

Many problems in the garden can be traced back to incorrect watering—either not enough or too much water. Many of the plants listed in this book grow quickly and require a large amount of water. Often, containers need to be watered every day. You will need to:

- **Check your containers frequently.** Dip your finger into the soil an inch or so, and if it feels dry, it's time to water. Use a moisture meter to give you a more exact idea of how wet the roots are.
- **Pay attention to your plants.** Your plants will tell you if their water needs aren't being met. Droopy, wilted leaves are a sign you waited too long to water. For other signs, see the "Troubleshooting Advice" table in Appendix A.
- **Be careful to water the soil, not the plant.** Plants absorb water through their roots in the soil, not through their leaves. Water left on a plant's leaves can cause diseases like powdery mildew.

- **Add a 1"–2" layer of mulch,** such as additional compost or straw, on top of the soil around plants once plants are growing. Adding mulch helps conserve moisture in the soil.

WHAT IS THE BEST WAY TO WATER PLANTS?

The ideal is a gentle shower of water that is slowly absorbed by the soil rather than a gush of water that displaces soil and exposes roots. Each time you water, water the container thoroughly until the entire root zone is wet and water begins to drain out of the bottom. Note: If the soil has dried out too much, water may drain out the bottom without being absorbed. If this happens to your soil, gently dig in the soil with a garden spade; don't turn the soil over, just loosen it. Next, repeatedly sprinkle the surface lightly with water. After several sprayings, the soil should begin to break up and loosen, allowing more water to be absorbed. Adding a 1"–2" layer of mulch can help prevent this in the future. Check that the top several inches are moist to ensure water is reaching the roots. If your container has a saucer underneath it, empty out the saucer (if possible) after you water. Sitting water doesn't allow roots to breathe and is a breeding ground for insects.

WHAT IS THE BEST TIME OF DAY TO WATER?

Watering in the morning prepares the plant for the day to come. When you water in the morning, less water evaporates than when you water during the heat of the day. The plant's leaves also have time to dry before the sun goes down, which helps prevent fungal diseases. If you have to water in the evening, take care not to get water on the leaves.

USE WATERING ASSISTANTS

If you are unable to water each day, consider adding an olla to your container when you plant (see "Watering Concerns" in Chapter 2). Water the container thoroughly and, at the same time, fill the olla with water. This allows you to go a little longer between watering than containers without ollas. During the warmest months of the year in hot climates, you may still have to water every day, but the plant roots have access to more water.

If you have a lot of containers, or if you travel frequently, consider using self-watering containers or adding some sort of automatic watering system. An automatic watering system can be as simple as a timer connected to a hose with driplines going to each container.

7. Feed Your Garden Regularly

Compost-rich potting soil will feed your garden for the first few weeks. Because frequent watering means nutrients are washed away (and roots can't go looking in the ground for additional nutrients), it's also a good idea to feed some plants as often as every week. Use a water-soluble organic fertilizer such as fish emulsion or liquid seaweed (or a combination of both). Follow dilution instructions on the bottle. If plants have specific

fertilizing requirements, they will be listed in the plant descriptions.

A quick note about fertilizer. Most fertilizers, including organic ones, list three numbers on the label. These numbers correlate to the amount of nitrogen, phosphorus, and potassium (N–P–K) provided by the fertilizer. These three elements are often used up by growing plants and need to be replenished.

8. Pay Attention to Your Containers Each Day

Make it a habit to spend some time in your garden each day. Daily watering needs will make this a necessity, but also use the time to observe what is going on with your plants. When checking your containers, do the following:

- Notice and enjoy the little things such as new growth and blossoms forming.
- Check under leaves for pests. Pests and disease are much easier to manage while they are small. See the "Quick Reference Guide for Organic Pest Control" table in Appendix A.
- Pull weeds promptly before they set seed. Container gardens usually have few weeds, and they are easily managed.
- Clean up fallen leaves and debris. Snip off spent blossoms. If a plant dies, remove it. It's important to keep your garden clean.

9. Harvest at the Right Time

This is the moment you've been waiting for! It's time to fill your harvest basket with the food grown in your garden. Read through the harvesting tips for each plant so you know the optimal time to harvest, usually when the crops are young and tender. Fruit and vegetables left too long on the plant can become tough or woody. Picking often encourages the plant to produce more crops. Use pruning shears to cut rather than tugging fruit and vegetables off the plant by hand.

10. Record Your Progress and Make a Plan for What to Plant Next

At the end of the growing season, when the plants are spent and the harvests are over, take time to record your experiences. Note the types of seeds or transplants you used, the date(s) you planted, what the harvests were like, and any challenges you faced. Mistakes are often the best teacher. Documenting your journey helps you learn.

If you are going to plant in the same container again, start over with fresh potting soil. Put plants and spent potting soil in the compost pile, but dispose of diseased or infected plants. Clean and disinfect the container using soapy water with a little bleach added. Begin again at Step 2, "Decide What You Are Going to Plant," and complete the steps again.

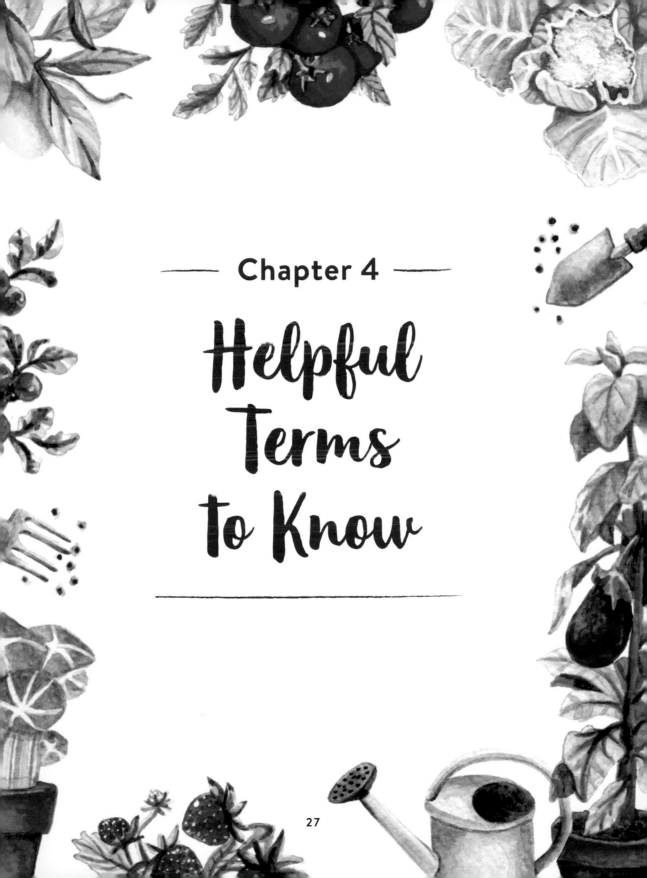

Chapter 4

Helpful Terms to Know

As you read through the plant listings, you may come across words and gardening terms you aren't familiar with. Here you'll find a listing of gardening terms you'll need to know.

AIRFLOW

Proper spacing between and around plants allows air to circulate and prevents mold and moisture-related diseases. Airflow around plants is as important as sunshine and water.

ANNUAL

A plant that completes its life cycle from seed to flower to production of seeds within one growing season, after which the entire plant dies. Examples of annual plants include basil, peas, and sunflowers.

BARE-ROOT

Dormant plant sold with roots exposed rather than in a container with soil. When purchasing and planting a bare-root plant, note that roots should be kept moist until they can be planted in soil.

BIENNIAL

A plant that requires 2 years to complete its life cycle from seed to flower to production of seeds followed by the plant's death. Examples of biennials include carrots, onions, and parsley.

BOLT

When a plant is under stress from lack of water, temperature, or other environmental factors, the plant may prematurely produce a flowering stem that produces seeds. Once a plant bolts, it often becomes inedible and bitter. Plants that may bolt include lettuce, cilantro, spinach, arugula, and celery.

BULB

Storage structure that contains the complete life cycle of a plant. Remains dormant until conditions are favorable for growth. Examples of bulbs include garlic and onions.

CHILL HOURS

The minimum period of cold weather a fruit-bearing tree needs to blossom and produce fruit. Cold climates have more chill hours than warm climates.

COCONUT COIR

A product made from the fiber of coconut shells and typically sold as pressed bricks; a common ingredient in many potting soils. Coconut coir allows for water retention, drainage, and aeration for roots. Coconut coir is a renewable resource.

COMPANION PLANTING

The practice of planting different crops in close proximity to benefit both crops in various ways, including increasing productivity, pest control, and pollination.

COMPOST

Decayed organic matter used as a soil conditioner or plant fertilizer.

CROSS-POLLINATION

Certain types of fruit trees need a second variety of fruit nearby to increase pollination and yield. For example, many blueberries do better when two different varieties are planted near each other.

CUT-AND-COME-AGAIN METHOD

This method is a way to harvest continually (typically by harvesting the outer leaves) from a single plant over several weeks or months, rather than harvesting the entire plant. Applies to plants such as arugula, celery, kale, lettuce, spinach, and Swiss chard.

DEADHEADING

The practice of removing faded blooms from flowers to encourage more blooms.

DECIDUOUS

A type of tree or shrub that sheds its leaves each year, usually in the autumn. A fig tree is an example of a deciduous tree.

DIVIDING

Dividing a plant means digging it up and dividing it into two or more sections. Each section should contain roots and part of the plant. These sections can be planted and become new plants.

DORMANCY

The period of time when perennial plants' growth and activity is at a minimum, normally during temperature extremes.

DWARF

Smaller and more compact than the typical variety for that type of plant. Fruit is usually normal size.

EVERGREEN

A plant or tree that retains its leaves throughout the year and into the following growing season. A citrus tree is an example of an evergreen tree.

FROST DATE

Date of the average first or average last freeze that occurs in spring or fall.

FROST-HARDY

A plant that can survive a certain amount of freezing temperatures without damage to leaves, stems, or roots.

FROST-SENSITIVE

A plant likely to be damaged or killed by freezing temperatures.

FULL SUN

For the purposes of this book, full sun is at least 6 hours of unobstructed sunlight each day.

GERMINATION

The development of a plant from a seed into a seedling in response to warmth, water, and sometimes light.

GROWING SEASON

The period of time during the year when conditions are right for plants to grow. Sometimes counted from the date of last frost in the spring to the first frost in the fall.

HAND POLLINATION

Assisting with the transfer of pollen in plants from the male reproductive organ (stamen) to the female reproductive organ (pistil) to form fruit. Use a small paintbrush to transfer the pollen or remove the male blossom (long, thin stem) and lightly touch the center of the male flower to the center of the female flower (bulbous stem).

HARDINESS ZONE

The geographical zone where certain plants grow best in that particular climate.

MULCH

A layer of material spread over the surface of the soil. Types of organic mulch for containers include leaves, grass clippings, peat moss, compost, straw, and pine needles. Organic mulch reduces evaporation, regulates temperature, and reduces weeds.

NITROGEN

An ingredient in most fertilizers that is crucial for healthy leafy growth. Plants use more nitrogen than any other nutrient. The amount of nitrogen is listed as the first number in the series of three numbers on fertilizers (N-P-K).

OLLA

A clay pot with a narrow neck and bulging body used as a watering technique that reduces evaporation and makes water available where it is needed by the roots. The wider part of the olla is buried in the soil with the narrow opening remaining above soil level. The olla is regularly filled with water, which seeps out through the porous wall of the pot into the surrounding soil and root zone of the plant.

ORGANIC FERTILIZER

Naturally occurring fertilizers derived from rock, animal, and plant matter. Liquid fish and seaweed are effective organic fertilizers for container gardening.

ORGANIC GARDENING

Gardening without synthetic pesticides and fertilizers in an effort to maintain plant and soil health.

PARTIAL SHADE

For the purposes of this book, partial shade is between 4–6 hours of unobstructed sunlight each day.

PEAT MOSS

Partially decomposed remains of sphagnum moss; used as a common ingredient in potting soil. Peat moss holds water and air, decomposes slowly, improves the texture, and raises the pH of the soil mix. Usually considered a less sustainable option than coconut coir.

PERENNIAL

A plant that lives for many growing seasons. The top of the plant may die back in the winter and come back each spring from the existing roots. Or the plant may keep its leaves year-round. Examples of perennials include blueberries, chives, citrus trees, fig trees, and rosemary.

PERLITE

A material formed when volcanic rock is crushed and heated; used as a common ingredient in potting soil. Perlite keeps soil loose and helps with water retention. Perlite retains less water than vermiculite.

PHOSPHORUS

An ingredient in most fertilizers that encourages strong root growth as well as the development of flowers, fruits, and seeds. The amount of phosphorus is listed as the second number in the series of three numbers on fertilizers (N-P-K).

PHOTOSYNTHESIS

The process whereby plants use sunlight to turn carbon dioxide into usable energy for the plant.

PLANT FAMILIES

Most crops are divided into different plant families that have similar growth requirements and habits. For example:

Alliums: garlic, onions, chives

Amaranths: beets, chard, spinach

Asters: lettuce, sunflowers, chamomile

Brassicas: broccoli, cabbage, cauliflower, kale, kohlrabi, radish

Cucurbits: squash, cucumber

Legumes: beans, peas

Mint: basil, mint, rosemary, sage

Nightshades: tomatoes, peppers, potatoes, eggplant

Umbels: carrots, celery, cilantro, dill, parsley

PLANTING GUIDE

A guide that tells the optimal time to plant vegetables, herbs, and flowers based on a specific location and/or climate.

POLLINATION

The transfer of pollen in plants from the male reproductive organ (stamen) to the female reproductive organ (pistil) to form fruit. Some flowering crops have separate male and female blossoms (squash, cucumber) while other crops (tomatoes, eggplant, peppers) have perfect flowers (both male and female organs in one flower). Bees and other pollinators assist in pollination by transferring the pollen from one flower to another or vibrating the flower to distribute the pollen inside the flower.

POTASSIUM

An ingredient in most fertilizers that increases the yield and quality of plants and helps plants resist disease and stress. The amount of potassium is listed as the last number in the series of three numbers on fertilizers (N-P-K).

POTTING SOIL

A sterile, lightweight blend of ingredients that holds moisture around plants' roots, provides air for growing roots, and allows for drainage for plants in containers. Sometimes called potting medium, container soil, or container mix. Look for vermiculite or perlite, and coconut coir or peat moss in the ingredients.

RESEED

The dropped seed from an annual plant that regrows the following season if conditions are right for germination and growth.

RHIZOMES

Fleshy stems that spread horizontally underground and contain several buds or growing points. Examples of rhizomes include ginger and turmeric.

ROOT CROWN

The area of the plant or tree where the roots branch off from the stem or trunk. It is very important not to bury this part of the plant when potting up trees and bushes.

ROOT ZONE

The area of soil, water, and oxygen below ground and around the roots of the plant that supplies the plant with water and nutrients.

SEEDLING

The first emergence of growth from seed. Emerging leaves are called cotyledons, while subsequent leaves are referred to as true leaves.

SELF-FRUITFUL

Fruit trees that do not require pollination from a different variety of tree. For example, most citrus trees are self-fruitful.

SELF-WATERING CONTAINERS

Containers with a water reservoir and wicking system that when kept full allow for a consistent source of moisture for plants. They should have an overflow mechanism that allows water to drain to prevent overfilling. Self-watering containers are helpful if you cannot water your containers each day, for plants that need a consistent level of moisture such as tomatoes, and in hot climates where containers dry out quickly.

SOIL PH

The measure of the acidity or alkalinity of the soil measured in pH units. The pH scale goes from 0 to 14. A pH of 7 is considered neutral. As the number increases, so does the alkalinity. As the number decreases, the acidity increases. Each plant has a preferred pH range. The pH level affects which nutrients are made available to the plant in the soil.

SUCCESSION PLANTING

The practice of staggering plantings throughout the growing season to ensure a continual harvest, rather than harvesting all at once.

THINNING

The removal of some plants to make room for the remaining plants to have enough soil, sunlight, water, and airflow to grow well. Thinning usually occurs once plants have two sets of true leaves.

TRANSPIRATION

The process of plants breathing in water from the soil through their roots and out through their leaves.

TRANSPLANT

A young plant that is somewhat past seedling stage; also called *starts*. Transplants usually have several sets of true leaves.

USDA PLANTING ZONE

System developed as a guide for planting and gardening. Divides the United States into thirteen zones by lowest annual temperatures. A plant's "hardiness zone" is the lowest USDA zone that it can withstand without dying.

VERMICULITE

Common ingredient in potting soil. A silicate material similar to mica. Vermiculite absorbs water, makes soil loose and friable, and adds a small amount of potassium, calcium, and magnesium. Vermiculite retains more water than perlite.

VINING PLANT

Plant that produces climbing or trailing stems from a central point or several points. Vines often require support or a trellis.

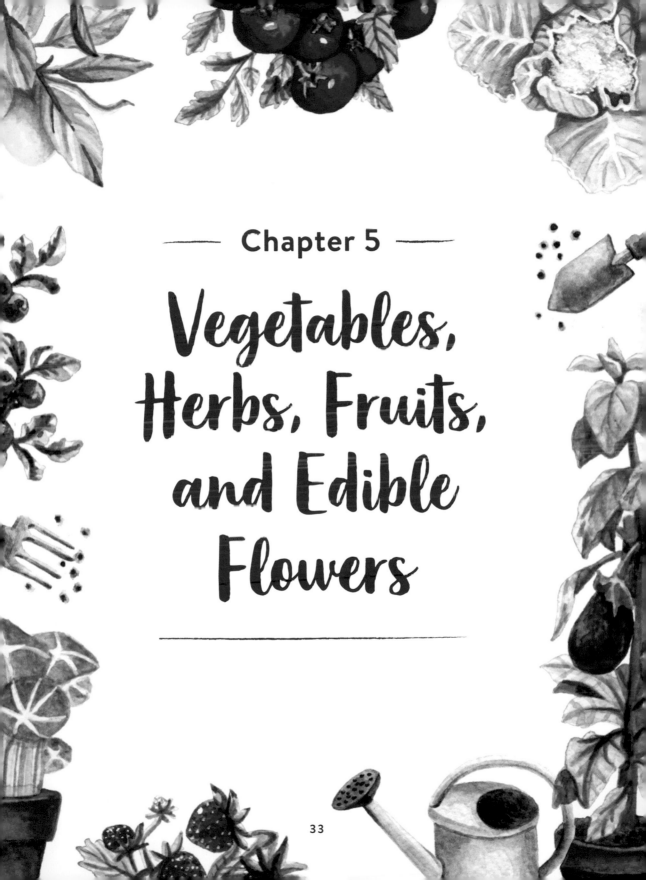

Chapter 5

Vegetables, Herbs, Fruits, and Edible Flowers

ARUGULA

Fast-growing, cool-season leafy green with tender leaves and a peppery flavor. Also called roquette or rocket.

DAYS TO HARVEST 35–50

SIZE 6"–12" tall and wide

DIFFICULTY Level 1: Easy

Good to Know

Arugula is an excellent container plant. Warm temperatures cause arugula to bolt and produce flowers. Once arugula bolts, the flavor is stronger and more bitter. The leaves and flowers of arugula are both edible. Good companions for arugula include beets, onions, carrots, cucumbers, and spinach.

How to Grow Arugula

CONTAINER SIZE Extra-small (or larger, see "Container Sizes" in Chapter 2).

WHEN TO PLANT Begin planting in the spring after last spring frost. Plant again in the fall to harvest in cooler months. Succession-plant arugula seeds every 2–3 weeks throughout the growing season for a fresh supply of arugula all season long.

VARIETIES TO TRY Astro (heat tolerant with mild flavor); Rocket (most common variety); Selvatica.

GROWS BEST FROM Seed.

HOW TO PLANT Plant seeds ¼" deep and 1"–3" apart. Thin seedlings to 6" apart.

LIGHT Full sun to partial shade. Provide shade during hot weather to prolong harvest and prevent bolting.

WATER Water well until plant is established and then provide regular water. Arugula grows well with an olla or in a self-watering container.

FEED Does not require supplemental feeding.

WHEN TO HARVEST Harvest when leaves are 4"–6" long. Harvest the entire plant by cutting at dirt level, or pick individual leaves from the outside of the plant. The plant will continue to produce leaves from the inside out.

Tips Flea beetles can damage arugula. Cover with garden fabric to prevent. See Appendix A for organic pest control options.

BASIL

Versatile, warm-season aromatic herb grown for its leaves.

DAYS TO HARVEST 30 days from transplant; 60–90 days from seed

SIZE 12"–24" tall and wide, depending on variety

DIFFICULTY Level 1: Easy

Good to Know

Basil is cold-sensitive and does not like temperatures below 50°F. Good companion plants include tomatoes and peppers. Look for compact varieties for containers.

How to Grow Basil

🪴 **CONTAINER SIZE** Extra-small (or larger, see "Container Sizes" in Chapter 2).

1️⃣ **WHEN TO PLANT** Basil needs warm soil to grow well. Plant after last spring frost date; ideal soil temperature for planting is 65°F–70°F.

🌿 **VARIETIES TO TRY** Genovese (best for pesto); Cinnamon; Mrs. Burns' Lemon; Thai; Holy.

🌱 **GROWS BEST FROM** Seed or transplant. Grow from seeds to try different varieties.

🌾 **HOW TO PLANT** Plant seeds ¼" deep and 2"–4" apart. Keep seeds moist until they sprout. Once plants are 2"–3" tall, thin to 6"–12" apart, depending on variety. Plant transplants at the same depth as nursery pots and space plants about 12" apart.

☀️ **LIGHT** Full sun. Partial shade in hot summer climates creates larger leaves.

💧 **WATER** Water well until plant is established and then allow basil to dry out a little between waterings to improve flavor.

⚗️ **FEED** Benefits from a liquid organic fertilizer application once or twice during the growing season.

🌱 **WHEN TO HARVEST** Harvest leaves anytime once the plant reaches 4"–6" tall.

Tips To encourage new growth and bushy plants, pinch basil back to just above sets of two leaves when the plant is 4"–6" tall. To retain the best flavor and encourage growth, do not let basil flower; continue to cut flowers back to just above two sets of leaves.

Tips for Growing Indoors Ideal indoor temperature for basil is 75°F–85°F. Provide supplemental lighting. Set a timer to run the light for 14–18 hours with the light about 2"–4" away from the plant. If seedlings are leggy, they need more light (change location or put grow lights closer to leaves). Keep evenly moist.

BEANS (BUSH)

Warm-season legume grown for tender pods. Bush beans are prolific and easy to grow in containers.

DAYS TO HARVEST 50–55

SIZE 6"–12" tall and 12"–18" wide

DIFFICULTY Level 1: Easy

Good to Know

Good companions for beans include carrots, cucumbers, and strawberries. Do not plant beans with onions. Bush beans produce a harvest over a 2-week period, with one larger crop followed by a smaller harvest a couple of weeks later.

How to Grow Beans

CONTAINER SIZE Medium (or larger, see "Container Sizes" in Chapter 2).

WHEN TO PLANT Beans need warm soil to sprout and grow well. Begin planting in the spring after last spring frost. Seeds will germinate more quickly in soil temperatures of 70°F–90°F. Succession-plant bean seeds every 2 weeks throughout the growing season for a fresh supply of beans all season long.

VARIETIES TO TRY Jade; Royal Burgundy; Provider; Gold Rush.

GROWS BEST FROM Seeds planted directly in the soil. Beans do not transplant well.

HOW TO PLANT Plant seeds 1" deep and 3"–4" apart. Keep seeds moist until they sprout.

LIGHT Full sun.

WATER Water well until plant is established and then provide regular water. Do not get water on leaves. Beans grow well with an olla or in a self-watering container.

FEED Benefits from a half-strength application of liquid organic fertilizer every 2 weeks during the growing season.

WHEN TO HARVEST Harvest beans when pods are firm and about the diameter of a pencil. Pick beans when young for best flavor. Harvest beans often to encourage production. Leaving beans on the plant signals the plant to stop producing.

Tips Aphids can be a problem. See Appendix A for organic pest control options.

BEETS

Colorful, cool-season crop grown for its bulbous root and tasty leaves.

DAYS TO HARVEST 45–65

SIZE 12" tall and 3"–4" wide

DIFFICULTY Level 1: Easy

Good to Know

Each beet "seed" is actually a cluster of seeds. Beets emerge as a clump that should be thinned once seedlings are 2"–3" tall. Beets are mostly pest- and disease-free. Beets become woody in hot weather or when they dry out. Good companions for beets include kohlrabi, lettuce, and beans.

How to Grow Beets

CONTAINER SIZE Small (or larger, see "Container Sizes" in Chapter 2). Container should be at least 10"–12" deep.

WHEN TO PLANT Begin planting in the spring 3–4 weeks before last spring frost date. Beets can also be planted in the fall in most climates. Succession-plant beet seeds every 2–3 weeks throughout the growing season for a fresh supply of beets all season long.

VARIETIES TO TRY Early Wonder (good choice for small beets and greens); Golden (yellow beet); Chiogga (striped variety).

GROWS BEST FROM Seed. Can transplant young seedlings.

HOW TO PLANT Plant seeds ½" deep and 3"–4" apart. Keep seeds moist until they sprout. Separate small seedlings and plant 3"–4" apart.

LIGHT Full sun to partial shade.

WATER Water well until plant is established and then provide regular water. Do not let beets dry out. Beets grow well with an olla or in a self-watering container.

FEED Benefits from a liquid organic fertilizer application each week during the growing season.

WHEN TO HARVEST Harvest the young and tender leaves anytime. For best flavor, harvest beets when they are about 1½" in diameter.

Tips Remove damaged leaves as they grow. Beets have the best flavor when they grow fast. Provide steady moisture and regular fertilizer for the best-tasting beets. Leave 1" of greens on the beet when trimming to prevent "bleeding."

BLUEBERRIES

Cold-hardy, perennial shrub with shiny oval leaves grown for its clusters of juicy, deep blue berries.

DAYS TO HARVEST Up to 3 years after planting

SIZE 2'–5' tall and wide, depending on variety

DIFFICULTY Level 3: Difficult

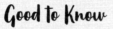
Good to Know

Blueberries grow well in containers. They often need a second plant for cross-pollination and to increase yield. Blueberries need acid-loving soil to grow well; amend the potting soil with additional peat moss or use potting soil formulated for acid-loving plants. Blueberries need a certain period of cold temperatures (chill hours) to produce fruit. Choose a container or dwarf type suited for your climate and zone.

How to Grow Blueberries

CONTAINER SIZE Extra-large (see "Container Sizes" in Chapter 2). Container should be at least 2' wide and 2' deep. A half-whiskey barrel is a good choice for growing blueberries. Place on a plant dolly before filling with soil so container can be moved to sheltered location during the coldest months of the year.

WHEN TO PLANT In the spring, after danger of frost has passed.

VARIETIES TO TRY Top Hat (bred for containers, good in cold regions); Earliblue (cold-hardy); Sunshine Blue (compact variety good for warm climates).

GROWS BEST FROM Bare-root bush or potted shrub. Choose a healthy plant with multiple stems.

HOW TO PLANT Fill container halfway with soil; set the bare-root bush in place with its roots spread out. If planting from a container, loosen compacted roots but keep root ball intact. Fill container with soil to same level of nursery pot. Do not bury the root crown.

LIGHT Full sun; may need shade during the hottest times of day in warm climates.

WATER Blueberries need consistent moisture but will not tolerate standing water. Well-draining soil is essential for growing blueberries; ensure your container has plenty of drainage holes. Adding a light layer of mulch (pine needles, moss, or bark) helps keep soil from drying out.

FEED Feed blueberries with a fertilizer for acid-loving plants each month during the growing season.

WHEN TO HARVEST Berries turn from green to deep blue. Ripe berries should taste sweet, not too tart. Blueberries on the plant ripen over the course of 2–3 weeks.

Tips Remove flowers the first year or two after planting to encourage root growth and strong plants. Cover container with tulle or bird netting just before berries begin to ripen to protect berries from birds. In very cold climates, protect roots from freezing temperatures by moving containers to a sheltered location out of the wind. Each spring, lightly prune the dead wood.

BORAGE

Large annual herb with beautiful blue flowers and grayish leaves. Flowers and leaves have mild cucumber flavor.

DAYS TO HARVEST 50–60 days from seed

SIZE 2'–3' tall and 12"–20" wide; size of container will limit size of borage

DIFFICULTY Level 1: Easy

Good to Know

Borage attracts bees and other beneficial insects. Borage plants grow large, so grow plants alone in their own container. It reseeds easily. Borage tolerates shade, sun, poor soil, and is drought-resistant. Good companions for borage in neighboring containers include strawberries and fruit trees.

How to Grow Borage

- **CONTAINER SIZE** Small (or larger, see "Container Sizes" in Chapter 2).

- **WHEN TO PLANT** Plant after last spring frost date. Ideal soil temperature for planting is 70°F.

- **VARIETIES TO TRY** (Regular) borage; try Alba for white blossoms.

- **GROWS BEST FROM** Seed. Borage has a large taproot and does best directly sown.

- **HOW TO PLANT** Plant seeds ¼"–½" deep directly in container. Thin to one plant when seedlings are several inches tall.

- **LIGHT** Full sun.

- **WATER** Water well until plant is established and then let top inch of soil dry out a little between waterings. The more water borage gets, the larger it will become.

- **FEED** Does not require supplemental feeding.

- **WHEN TO HARVEST** Harvest new leaves before bristles develop. Pick new flowers as soon as they appear; keep flowers picked to encourage production.

Tips Pinch back seedling when it is 6" tall to encourage a bushier plant with more flowers. Trim back borage for size as desired. Cut back regularly to encourage new growth. Leave a few flowers on the plant to save seeds from at the end of the season. Borage seeds develop inside the flowerhead after the blooms wither and fall off. Collect the seeds once they turn black.

BROCCOLI

Cool-weather, frost-hardy member of the brassica family grown for its edible flower buds and stalk.

DAYS TO HARVEST 100–150 days from seed; 55–80 days from transplant

SIZE 18"–24" tall and wide

DIFFICULTY Level 1: Easy

Good to Know

Broccoli plants can get large. Look for compact varieties that grow well in containers. Broccoli grown during cool weather will have a sweeter flavor than its warm-weather counterpart. Good companions for broccoli include dill, chamomile, sage, beets, and onions.

How to Grow Broccoli

CONTAINER SIZE Medium (or larger, see "Container Sizes" in Chapter 2). Container should be 10"–12" deep.

WHEN TO PLANT Begin planting in the spring 5 weeks before last spring frost date. Broccoli can also be planted in the fall in many climates.

VARIETIES TO TRY Munchkin (small variety that grows well in containers); De Cicco (fast-maturing variety).

GROWS BEST FROM Seed or transplant. When choosing transplants at the nursery, look for compact green leaves on a short stem.

HOW TO PLANT Plant seeds ¼" deep and 3" apart. Thin to 12"–20" apart when seedlings are 2"–3" apart. Plant transplants 12"–20" apart, and a little deeper than nursery-pot level, but not any deeper than the first set of leaves.

LIGHT Full sun.

WATER Water well until plants are established and then provide regular water. Broccoli grows well with an olla or in a self-watering container.

FEED Benefits from a liquid organic fertilizer application each week, 3–4 weeks after planting.

WHEN TO HARVEST Harvest broccoli when the head is full and tight and when the buds are dark green and not opening. If they turn yellow, you've waited too long. Harvest broccoli before temperatures are consistently above 75°F. Pick it in the morning for best flavor. Use a sharp knife to cut stalk off at an angle 5"–8" below the head. Cutting at an angle allows water to drain off rather than puddling on the remaining stem. Most broccoli varieties produce smaller side shoots after the main stalk is harvested. Harvest side shoots 2–3 weeks later.

Tips Insects such as cabbage worms, cutworms, snails, and slugs can ruin young broccoli plants. See Appendix A for organic pest control options.

CABBAGE

Cool-season vegetable in the brassica family grown for edible head composed of layers of thick leaves.

DAYS TO HARVEST 80–180 days from seed; 65–105 days from transplant

SIZE 12"–18" tall and 18"–24" wide

DIFFICULTY Level 2: Medium

Good to Know

Cabbage likes cool but not freezing temperatures. It will not form a head but will instead split or bolt if exposed to too much heat or severe frost. Good companions for cabbage include thyme, dill, chamomile, sage, and onions.

How to Grow Cabbage

CONTAINER SIZE Medium (or larger, see "Container Sizes" in Chapter 2). Container should be 10"–12" deep.

WHEN TO PLANT Begin planting in the spring 5 weeks before last spring frost date. Cabbage can also be planted in the fall in many climates.

VARIETIES TO TRY Savoy Ace (compact curly variety); Early Jersey Wakefield (compact green variety); Red Acre (compact red variety).

GROWS BEST FROM Seed or transplant. When choosing transplants at the nursery, look for small transplants with compact green leaves on a short stem.

HOW TO PLANT Plant seeds ¼" deep and 3" apart. Thin to 12"–20" apart when seedlings are 2"–3" tall. Plant transplants 12"–20" apart a little deeper than nursery-pot level, but not deeper than the first set of leaves.

LIGHT Full sun.

WATER Water well until plants are established and then provide regular water. Cabbage grows well with an olla or in a self-watering container. Once cabbage is almost full-size, cut back a little on watering to prevent the head from splitting.

FEED Benefits from a liquid organic fertilizer application each week, 3–4 weeks after planting.

WHEN TO HARVEST Harvest cabbage when heads are well formed and firm, cutting off at the base with a sharp knife. Young, small heads have the best flavor.

Tips Cut away the large bottom leaves if they turn yellow. Insects such as cabbage worms, cutworms, snails, and slugs can ruin young cabbage leaves. See Appendix A for organic pest control options.

CALENDULA

Easy-to-grow, cool-season annual flower with daisy-like petals that attracts bees and butterflies to your garden. Calendula petals can be eaten fresh in salads, as a garnish, or dried and made into tea.

DAYS TO HARVEST 50–55

SIZE 12"–24" tall and wide

DIFFICULTY Level 1: Easy

Good to Know

Also called pot marigold, calendula is used to make skin salves and ointments. Blooms open each day with the sun and then close at night. A cool-loving flower, it reseeds easily. Sometimes grown as a trap crop for aphids and other pests. Good companion for carrots, cucumbers, peas, and tomatoes.

How to Grow Calendula

CONTAINER SIZE Extra-small (or larger, see "Container Sizes" in Chapter 2).

WHEN TO PLANT Begin planting after last spring frost.

VARIETIES TO TRY Pacific Beauty (has large blooms); Orange Button (has double blooms and dark centers).

GROWS BEST FROM Seed or transplant. Look for small transplants; they will adjust better to planting.

HOW TO PLANT Plant seeds directly in containers about ¼" deep. Germination usually takes 7–10 days. Thin plants 6"–12" apart when they are 1"–2" tall. Plant transplants at the same depth as nursery pots and space plants 6"–12" apart.

LIGHT Full sun.

WATER Water well until plant is established and then provide regular water.

FEED Does not require supplemental feeding.

WHEN TO HARVEST Harvest blooms when petals begin to open. Leave a small amount of stem attached to the flower to hold bloom together. Only the petals are edible; do not eat the flower centers.

Tips Deadhead the plant to get more blooms. Succession-plant every 2–3 weeks for a continual harvest.

CARROTS

Adaptable root vegetable with delicious flavor and texture that grows well in containers in just about every climate.

DAYS TO HARVEST 60–100

SIZE 6"–12" tall and wide

DIFFICULTY Level 2: Medium

Good to Know

Carrots do best when grown in a container by themselves or with other faster-growing root vegetables, such as radishes. Carrot seeds take 10 days to germinate and must remain moist until they sprout. Hot weather causes carrots to become fibrous. A frost often improves the taste of carrots. Good companions include tomatoes, lettuce, chives, onions, radishes, and sage.

How to Grow Carrots

CONTAINER SIZE Small (or larger, see "Container Sizes" in Chapter 2). Container should be at least 8" deep; 10"–12" deep is even better.

WHEN TO PLANT Begin planting in the spring 3 weeks before last spring frost date. Succession-plant carrots every 3 weeks for a continual harvest. Carrots can also be planted in the fall in most climates.

VARIETIES TO TRY Scarlet Nantes; Danvers Half Long; Little Fingers; Chantenay.

GROWS BEST FROM Seeds planted directly in containers.

HOW TO PLANT Carefully plant the small seeds about ½" apart and cover lightly with soil. Keep soil moist for 10 days until seeds germinate. Thin carrot seedlings by clipping with pruning snips (rather than pulling) to 2" apart when they are about 4" tall.

LIGHT Full sun to partial shade.

WATER Water well until plants are established and then provide regular water. Carrots grow well in a self-watering container.

FEED Benefits from a liquid organic fertilizer application once or twice during the growing season.

WHEN TO HARVEST Gently pry soil from around the very top of the carrot when the stalks are thick and tall. If carrot is full-colored and about finger-size, gather greens together and pull. Carrots can be left in the ground for a few extra weeks; harvest carrots as needed.

Tips After harvesting, trim greens from carrots right away, as they take moisture away from the carrot.

CAULIFLOWER

Cool-weather vegetable in the brassica family grown for the (typically) white florets that make up the edible head.

DAYS TO HARVEST 60–100

SIZE 12" tall and 18"–24" wide

DIFFICULTY Level 2: Medium

Good to Know

Cauliflower grows best alone in its own container. It's trickier to grow than its relatives because it doesn't like conditions too hot or too cold. To grow cauliflower successfully, it needs at least 2 months of cool weather (60°F is ideal) to mature.

How to Grow Cauliflower

CONTAINER SIZE Medium (or larger, see "Container Sizes" in Chapter 2). Container should be 10"–12" deep.

WHEN TO PLANT Begin planting in the spring 4 weeks before last spring frost date. Cauliflower can also be planted in the fall in many climates. (Cover if frost is expected.)

VARIETIES TO TRY Snowball (white variety); Graffiti (bright purple head); Cheddar (orange head).

GROWS BEST FROM Seed or transplant. When choosing transplants at the nursery, look for compact green leaves on a short stem.

HOW TO PLANT Plant seeds ¼" deep and 6" apart. Thin to 12"–20" apart when seedlings are 2"–3" tall. Plant transplants a little deeper than nursery-pot level, but not deeper than the first set of leaves, and space plants 12"–20" apart. Handle transplants carefully; do not disturb roots.

LIGHT Full sun to partial shade.

WATER Water well until plants are established and then provide regular water. Cauliflower needs even watering; stress causes it to bolt. Do not let the plant dry out. Cauliflower grows well with an olla or in a self-watering container.

FEED Benefits from a liquid organic fertilizer application each week, 3–4 weeks after planting.

WHEN TO HARVEST When the head is about 6" across and buds are tight and unopened, it is time to harvest. Cut off at the base below the head with a sharp knife.

Tips Cauliflower heads in some varieties can discolor if they are exposed to sunlight. To prevent this, clip outer leaves together with a clothespin to cover head when cauliflower head is visible and about 2" wide. Clip loosely and check occasionally for pests and growth or to let the head dry out after a rain.

CELERY

Cool-loving, long-season vegetable grown for its stalks and leaves.

DAYS TO HARVEST 120–150

SIZE 12"–18" tall and 6"–12" wide

DIFFICULTY Level 2: Medium

Good to Know

Homegrown celery is flavorful and delicious. Celery is sensitive to hot and cold temperatures and will respond by bolting or going to seed. Celery requires consistent moisture and rich soil to grow well. It does best when grown by itself in a container.

How to Grow Celery

CONTAINER SIZE Small (or larger, see "Container Sizes" in Chapter 2).

WHEN TO PLANT Celery needs 4 months of cool weather. In cold areas, plant in the spring, 4 weeks before last spring frost. In warm areas, plant celery in late summer or fall.

VARIETIES TO TRY Tango; Utah.

GROWS BEST FROM Transplant will yield the fastest results. Celery seeds take a long time to germinate. You can also grow from cut-off ends of celery; this, too, takes longer than planting from transplant, and often the stalks are not as large.

HOW TO PLANT Plant transplants at the same depth as nursery pots and space plants 6"–8" apart.

LIGHT Full sun; partial shade in warmer climates.

WATER Water well until plant is established and then provide regular water. Do not let dry out. Celery grows well with an olla or in a self-watering container.

FEED Benefits from a half-strength application of liquid organic fertilizer every 2 weeks during the growing season.

WHEN TO HARVEST Harvest individual stalks around the outside of the plant as needed. Plant will continue to produce stalks. To harvest the entire stalk, cut across the base just below the soil line with a sharp knife. Heat makes celery bitter; harvest before temperatures climb above 70°F.

Tips Be diligent about watering. Celery that doesn't get enough water often has hollow stalks and is stringy.

CHAMOMILE

Annual and perennial herb with green fern-like leaves and white daisy-like flowers. Grown for the yellow center of its flowers. Makes a calming tea.

DAYS TO HARVEST 60–65

SIZE 8"–24" tall and wide, depending on the variety

DIFFICULTY Level 1: Easy

Good to Know
Chamomile grows well with most other herbs and vegetables. Excellent companions for chamomile include cabbage and onions. Reseeds easily.

How to Grow Chamomile

CONTAINER SIZE Extra-small (or larger, see "Container Sizes" in Chapter 2).

WHEN TO PLANT Begin planting German chamomile after last spring frost date. Wait to plant Roman chamomile until soil temperatures reach 45°F.

VARIETIES TO TRY German chamomile (a taller annual and best for tea); Roman chamomile (low-growing mounding perennial that can be used as a ground cover).

GROWS BEST FROM Seed or transplant. Look for small transplants; they will adjust better to planting.

HOW TO PLANT Scatter seeds on soil and press in gently; do not cover with soil. Seeds take 7–10 days to germinate. Keep seeds moist until they sprout. Thin seedlings to about 8" apart. Plant transplants at the same depth as nursery pots and space plants 8" apart.

LIGHT Give newly planted chamomile partial shade while roots are getting established. Once established, grow in full sun to partial shade.

WATER Water well until plant is established and then provide regular water. Chamomile grows well with an olla or in a self-watering container.

FEED Does not require supplemental feeding.

WHEN TO HARVEST Harvest flowers for tea when white petals begin to curl.

Tips Pull off white petals before the flowers dry to prevent damaging yellow centers. Spread flower centers on a tray and let dry in a warm location for a few days.

CHIVES

Hardy, easy-to-grow, cool-season perennial herb in the allium family, grown for its onion-flavored green stalks and purple flowers that develop from underground bulbs.

DAYS TO HARVEST 75–85 days from seed; 30 days from transplant

SIZE 12" tall and wide

DIFFICULTY Level 1: Easy

Good to Know

Chives are one of the easiest herbs to grow and a great choice for a beginning gardener. Chives are a perennial in most areas. Greens may die back in cold weather, but underground bulbs will send out new growth in the spring. All parts of the plant including the flowers are edible. Chives are a good companion plant with parsley, carrots, lettuce, peas, and cucumbers.

How to Grow Chives

CONTAINER SIZE Extra-small (or larger, see "Container Sizes" in Chapter 2). Container should be 6" deep.

WHEN TO PLANT Begin planting after last spring frost date. Ideal soil temperature for planting is 60°F–65°F.

VARIETIES TO TRY Fine Leaf (standard culinary variety); Garlic Chives (same family, but garlic flavor and more heat-tolerant).

 GROWS BEST FROM Seed or transplant.

HOW TO PLANT Plant four to six seeds ¼" deep and 6" apart directly in container. Keep seeds moist until they sprout. Thin to one to two plants 12" apart when several inches tall. Plant transplants at the same depth as nursery pot and space plants 12" apart.

LIGHT Full sun; partial shade in very hot climates.

WATER Water well until plant is established and then provide regular water. Not enough water will cause tips to brown. Chives grow well with an olla or in a self-watering container.

FEED Fertilize once a month during harvesting with a liquid organic fertilizer.

WHEN TO HARVEST Snip stems at base of plant, never harvesting more than one-third of the plant. New shoots will form in their place.

Tips Usually pest-free. Remove blossoms to prevent self-sowing. Plants are prolific and multiply readily; should be divided every few years. In cold areas, bring containers inside for winter or let them go dormant. Greens will die back in very hot or very cold weather and come back when temperatures cool or warm.

Tips for Growing Indoors Ideal indoor temperature for chives is 50°F–75°F. Provide supplemental lighting. Set a timer to run the light for 16–18 hours with the light about 6" away from the plant. Rotate plant each time you water to keep growth even. Water when top of soil is dry. Mist plant with water every few days to provide extra humidity.

CILANTRO

Cool-season, upright, bushy annual herb grown for citrus-tasting leaves (cilantro) or seeds (coriander), often used in Latin American and Asian cooking.

DAYS TO HARVEST 50–55 days (cilantro); 90–150 days (coriander)

SIZE 6"–28" tall and 4"–12" wide

DIFFICULTY Level 1: Easy

Good to Know

Cilantro prefers cooler weather and will bolt (go to seed) in warm weather. Choose slow-bolt varieties if growing for the leaves. Cilantro flowers attract many beneficial insects. Good companions for cilantro include parsley, dill, peas, and beans.

How to Grow Cilantro

CONTAINER SIZE Small (or larger, see "Container Sizes" in Chapter 2). Has a long taproot and does best in containers at least 12" deep.

WHEN TO PLANT Begin planting after last spring frost date. Ideal soil temperature for planting is 55°F–68°F. Succession-plant every 2 weeks for a continual harvest of the leaves.

VARIETIES TO TRY Santo; Calypso (good slow-bolt variety).

GROWS BEST FROM Seed or transplant. Look for small transplants; they will adjust better to planting. Cilantro grown from seed is less likely to bolt and go to seed.

HOW TO PLANT Plant seeds ¼"–1/2" deep and 3"–4" apart directly in container. Keep seeds moist until they sprout. Plant transplants at the same depth as nursery pots and space plants 3"–4" apart.

LIGHT Full sun to partial shade. In hot areas, provide afternoon shade; too much sun will cause cilantro to bolt sooner.

WATER Water well until plant is established and then provide regular water. Do not get water on leaves; can cause powdery mildew.

FEED Benefits from a half-strength application of liquid organic fertilizer every 2 weeks during the growing season.

WHEN TO HARVEST Harvest leaves after plant is 3"–6" tall. To harvest leaves, cut stalks at soil level. Seeds are ready to harvest when they turn brown.

Tips Remove yellow, wilted, or damaged leaves.

Tips for Growing Indoors Ideal indoor temperature for cilantro is 50°F–75°F. Provide supplemental lighting. Set a timer to run the light for 10–11 hours with the light about 6" away from the plant. Water only when top inch or so of soil is dry. Indoor-grown cilantro does best in an unglazed terra cotta pot.

CITRUS

Citrus trees have evergreen leaves and beautiful-smelling blossoms, and they bear full-size edible fruit.

DAYS TO HARVEST Up to 3 years after planting

SIZE 2'–5' tall and 3' wide, depending on variety

DIFFICULTY Level 2 or 3: Medium to Difficult, depending on your climate; easier to grow in warm climates

Good to Know

Citrus trees grow very well in containers. Choose a dwarf variety. Citrus grows best in subtropical climates with temperatures above freezing. In colder climates, bring citrus indoors during cold months. The sweetest varieties need very warm weather; sour types like lemon are good choices for cooler climates. Citrus fruit ripens over the course of 9 months to 1 year.

How to Grow Citrus

CONTAINER SIZE Extra-large (see "Container Sizes" in Chapter 2). Container should be at least 2' wide and 2' deep. A half-whiskey barrel or extra-large terra cotta pot is a good choice. Place on a plant dolly before filling with soil in cold climates so container can be moved to sheltered location during coldest months of the year.

WHEN TO PLANT In the spring, after danger of frost has passed.

VARIETIES TO TRY Dwarf Improved Meyer Lemon, Kumquat, and Calamondin are all more cold-hardy types good for containers.

GROWS BEST FROM Trees grafted onto dwarf rootstock and sold in containers. Look at roots and make sure they do not circle the nursery container. Look for healthy trees with shiny leaves.

HOW TO PLANT Fill container halfway with soil; set the tree in place. Loosen compacted roots lightly but keep root ball intact. Fill container with soil to same level of nursery pot. Do not bury the root crown or graft.

LIGHT Full sun; may need shade during the hottest times of day in warm climates.

WATER Water well until plant is established and then provide regular water. Let top couple of inches of soil dry out between waterings.

FEED Feed with a citrus fertilizer each month during the growing season.

WHEN TO HARVEST Taste is the best measure of when citrus is ripe. It is important to learn the approximate time when the type of citrus you are growing becomes ripe, and then begin sampling the fruit.

Tips Citrus grown in containers will need to be repotted to a larger container or have roots trimmed back every few years. In cooler climates, put containers next to a wall that gets reflected heat. All citrus is frost-tender and should be brought indoors in places where the nighttime temperatures are consistently below 35°F. Move back outside after danger of frost has passed in the spring.

CUCUMBER

Cucumbers are a warm-season, vining crop that love sun and water.

DAYS TO HARVEST 50–70

SIZE Vining plants can grow large (over 3' tall and wide); bush varieties are 1'–2' tall and wide

DIFFICULTY Level 1: Easy

Good to Know

Allow plenty of room for cucumber plants and provide a trellis for vining and bush plants to climb. Look for container, bush, or dwarf varieties. Good companions for cucumbers include beans, peas, radishes, and sunflowers.

How to Grow Cucumbers

CONTAINER SIZE Medium (or larger, see "Container Sizes" in Chapter 2). Container should be at least 10" deep.

WHEN TO PLANT Begin planting in the spring 1–2 weeks after last spring frost and the soil temperature reaches 70°F.

VARIETIES TO TRY Salad Bush and Spacemaster (both have full-size cucumbers on small plants); Lemon (round yellow fruits; requires trellis).

GROWS BEST FROM Seed or transplant. When choosing transplants at the nursery, look for compact green leaves and young plants.

HOW TO PLANT Plant a group of three seeds 1" deep and 12" apart. When seedlings have three leaves, thin to one plant every 12". Plant transplants at the same depth as nursery pots and space plants 12" apart.

LIGHT Full sun.

WATER Water well until plant is established and then provide regular water. Cucumbers grow well with an olla or in a self-watering container. Do not let the plants dry out, or cucumbers will be bitter and hollow.

FEED Benefits from a liquid organic fertilizer application each week during the growing season.

WHEN TO HARVEST For best taste, harvest cucumbers when young and blossom flower is still attached. Leaving cucumbers on the vine too long signals the plant to stop producing. Cut (don't pull) cucumbers off the vine.

Tips Mulch soil to prevent container from drying out. Male flowers appear first, followed by female flowers, which have a bulbous stem. If female flowers do not produce fruit, consider hand-pollinating female blossoms with pollen from the male. Avoid getting water on the leaves to prevent powdery mildew. Look for disease-resistant varieties if disease has been an issue in the past. See Appendix A for organic pest control options.

DILL

Frost-sensitive, annual herb grown for fragrant leaves and seeds.

DAYS TO HARVEST 40–60 days (fronds harvest); 85–115 days (seed harvest)

SIZE 18"–4' tall, depending on variety; usually 12" wide

DIFFICULTY Level 1: Easy

Good to Know

Dill likes warm soil. Attracts many beneficial insects such as ladybugs and lacewings. Good companions for dill include cabbage, lettuce, onions, and cucumbers.

How to Grow Dill

CONTAINER SIZE Small (or larger, see "Container Sizes" in Chapter 2). Has a long taproot and does best in containers at least 12" deep.

WHEN TO PLANT Begin planting after last spring frost date. Ideal soil temperature for planting is 65°F–70°F. Succession-plant every 3 weeks for a continual harvest of the leaves.

VARIETIES TO TRY Fernleaf (only 6"–8" high; slow to bolt and excellent for containers); Bouquet (grown for large blooms and seeds for pickling).

GROWS BEST FROM Seed. If you use transplants, look for small ones (they will adjust better to planting). Dill grown from seed is less likely to bolt (go to seed).

HOW TO PLANT Plant seeds ⅛"–¼" deep directly in container. Thin seedlings to 4" apart. Keep seeds moist until they sprout. Plant transplants at the same depth as nursery pots and space plants 4" apart; handle roots very carefully.

LIGHT Full sun.

WATER Water well until plant is established and then let top inch of soil dry out a little between waterings.

FEED Does not require supplemental feeding.

WHEN TO HARVEST Harvest fronds as soon as plant is 5"–6" tall. Don't overcut until plant grows larger. Harvest seeds just as they turn from green to brown for best flavor.

Tips Allow plant to go to flower to attract beneficial insects to your garden.

Tips for Growing Indoors Ideal indoor temperature for dill is 60°F–80°F. Because dill can get large, choose a dwarf variety like Fernleaf when growing indoors. Provide supplemental lighting. Set a timer to run the light for 10–11 hours with the light about 6" away from the plant. Rotate plant each time you water to keep growth even. Water when top of soil is dry.

EGGPLANT

Heat-loving, frost-tender, long-season member of the nightshade family (potatoes, peppers, and tomatoes) grown for its smooth-skinned, spongy fruit.

DAYS TO HARVEST 70–120

SIZE 24"–30" tall and wide

DIFFICULTY Level 1: Easy

Good to Know

In cooler areas, growing eggplant in containers is more successful because containers heat up more quickly than in-ground garden beds. Eggplant plants can get large; look for dwarf varieties when growing in containers. Good companions include green beans, peppers, and okra.

How to Grow Eggplant

CONTAINER SIZE Medium (or larger, see "Container Sizes" in Chapter 2). Container should be at least 10" deep.

WHEN TO PLANT Begin planting in the spring 2 weeks after last spring frost.

VARIETIES TO TRY Bambino; Indian; Fairy Tale.

GROWS BEST FROM Transplant. Look for small, compact transplants without blossoms.

HOW TO PLANT Handle transplant roots carefully. Plant transplants at the same depth as nursery pots and space plants 12"–18".

LIGHT Full sun.

WATER Water well until plant is established and then provide regular water. Do not let dry out. Eggplants grow well with an olla or in a self-watering container.

FEED Benefits from a half-strength application of liquid organic fertilizer every 2 weeks during the growing season.

WHEN TO HARVEST Harvest fruits when small for best taste. An eggplant that is ready to harvest will have bright, shiny skin and feel firm and heavy for its size. Clip fruit from stem with hand pruners so as not to damage plant.

Tips Large plants may require staking. Flea beetles can damage eggplant. Cover with garden fabric to prevent. Colorado potato beetle can also be an issue; handpick the bugs off. See Appendix A for additional organic pest control options.

FIG TREE

Heat-loving, multibranched tree with large deciduous leaves grown for its sweet, teardrop-shaped fruit.

DAYS TO HARVEST Up to 3 years after planting

SIZE 6'–8' tall and wide

DIFFICULTY Level 2: Medium

Good to Know

Fig trees grow well in containers. In-ground fig trees grow large; growing fig trees in a container slows their growth. Fig trees prefer warm climates and sunny locations.

How to Grow Fig Tree

CONTAINER SIZE Extra-large (see "Container Sizes" in Chapter 2). Container should be at least 2' wide and 2' deep. A half-whiskey barrel is a good choice. Place on a plant dolly before filling with soil in cold climates so container can be moved to sheltered location during coldest months of the year.

WHEN TO PLANT In the spring, after danger of frost has passed.

VARIETIES TO TRY Black Mission (good for warm areas); Lattarula (good in cooler climates).

GROWS BEST FROM Bare-root or potted tree. Look at roots and make sure they do not circle the nursery container. Look for healthy trees with deep-green leaves.

HOW TO PLANT Fill container halfway with soil; set the bare-root tree in place with its roots spread out. If planting from a container, loosen compacted roots but keep root ball intact. Fill container with soil to same level of nursery pot. Do not bury the root crown.

LIGHT Full sun; may need shade during the hottest times of day in warm climates.

WATER Water deeply at planting. Monitor soil and water only when top inch or two is dry. Water container deeply and thoroughly. Frequent shallow watering will result in a poor root system.

FEED Benefits from a liquid organic fertilizer application at the beginning of the season and then every 2–3 weeks once fruits appear.

WHEN TO HARVEST Figs are ripe when the skin feels soft and changes color from green to yellow and then brown. (Color may vary, depending on variety.) Figs often have two crops each season; first crop in midseason on last year's wood and again in the fall on the current year's growth.

Tips In areas where winter temperatures go below 20°F, move to a sheltered location or indoors once the fig tree goes dormant (loses its leaves). Move it back outside in the spring.

GARLIC

Bulbous member of the allium family that can be harvested early as a milder-tasting green garlic or harvested later as garlic bulbs.

DAYS TO HARVEST 60 days (green garlic); up to 8 months (garlic bulbs)

SIZE 18"–24" tall and 3"–4" wide

DIFFICULTY Level 1: Easy

Good to Know

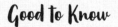

Garlic is well suited to growing in containers. Good companions for garlic include fruit trees and tomatoes. Do not plant near peas or beans.

How to Grow Garlic

CONTAINER SIZE Extra-small (or larger, see "Container Sizes" in Chapter 2). Container should be 6" deep.

WHEN TO PLANT Plant in the fall (in most areas) for garlic bulbs or in early spring for green garlic.

VARIETIES TO TRY Softneck varieties store longer and grow well in areas with hot summers and mild winters. Hardneck varieties grow best in cold climates.

GROWS BEST FROM Garlic cloves.

HOW TO PLANT Separate the cloves of a head of garlic and plant each clove (pointy side up) about 3" deep and 1"–2" apart for green garlic and 6" apart for garlic cloves.

LIGHT Full sun.

WATER Water well while new leaves are forming. When leaves begin to die back, water less often. Garlic grows well with an olla or in a self-watering container.

FEED Benefits from a liquid organic fertilizer application every other week during the growing season.

WHEN TO HARVEST Harvest green garlic as soon as 4–5 weeks after planting, when stalks are tall. Pull entire plant. Harvest garlic cloves when nearly all leaves have turned brown. Dig up garlic with a garden trowel rather than pulling.

Tips Garlic is a good companion plant for most crops (other than beans, peas, sage, and parsley); tuck a few plants around other vegetables to help deter pests.

GINGER

Heat-loving, tropical perennial herb grown for its bamboo-like leaves and flavorful rhizomes. Grown as a long-season annual in all but the warmest locations.

DAYS TO HARVEST 8–10 months

SIZE 2'–4' tall and 2'–3' wide

DIFFICULTY Level 2 or 3: Medium to Difficult, depending on your climate; easier to grow in warm climates

Good to Know

Ginger needs a long, warm growing season to grow well (zones 8 and above). In cooler climates (zones 7 and below), pre-sprout indoors (see directions that follow) 10 months before first fall frost date and then plant outside when the weather warms in the spring. Turmeric and ginger have similar growing requirements and can be near each other.

How to Grow Ginger

CONTAINER SIZE Medium (or larger, see "Container Sizes" in Chapter 2). Container should be at least 12" deep.

WHEN TO PLANT In the spring, after danger of frost has passed.

VARIETIES TO TRY Yellow Ginger Root (common ginger); Japanese Ginger (more cold-hardy; grown for flower buds).

GROWS BEST FROM Rhizomes. Look for light-colored, thin-skinned organic ginger that is plump and firm with several bumpy nodules. Cut rhizomes into 2" pieces, each piece containing two to three nodules. Allow cut ends to dry before planting.

HOW TO PLANT Pre-sprout rhizomes in cool climates by planting a rhizome 2" deep in 3½" pots on heat mats. Keep warm and slightly moist (but not soggy; it will rot). Once ginger sprouts, let it grow in a sunny spot until it is warm enough to plant outside. Gradually let plants become accustomed to outdoor conditions for a week and then carefully transplant sprouts to larger containers outdoors. In warmer areas with a longer growing season, plant rhizomes with nodules pointing up 2"–3" deep and 6"–8" apart.

LIGHT Although ginger needs warmth, it prefers partial shade, especially in warm-climate areas.

WATER Water well until plant is established and then provide regular water. Needs consistent moisture but not soggy soil.

FEED Benefits from a liquid seaweed fertilizer application every 2 weeks during the growing season.

WHEN TO HARVEST Harvest when leaves begin to yellow and die back, or before first fall frost. Dig down and carefully harvest rhizomes. Alternatively, dump container into a wheelbarrow to harvest rhizomes.

Tips Once temperatures dip below 50°F, bring ginger indoors if it is not ready to harvest. Give indoor-grown ginger warmth and sun exposure or provide supplemental lighting. The ideal indoor temperature for ginger is about 75°F.

GREEN ONIONS (SCALLIONS)

Long-stemmed member of the allium family harvested before the bulb matures and grown for edible green and white stem.

DAYS TO HARVEST 30–90 days, depending on planting method

SIZE 6"–12" tall and 1"–2" wide

DIFFICULTY Level 1: Easy

Good to Know
Green onions have the flavor of onions without the long wait in the garden. Green onions include scallions and spring onions, and all are a great choice for growing in containers. Onions are good companion plants for most crops (other than beans, peas, and sage); tuck a few plants around other vegetables to help deter pests.

How to Grow Green Onions

CONTAINER SIZE Extra-small (or larger, see "Container Sizes" in Chapter 2). Container should be 6" deep.

WHEN TO PLANT Begin planting 2 weeks before last spring frost date. For fall planting, plant seeds up to 4 weeks before the first fall frost.

VARIETIES TO TRY Evergreen Long White; White Lisbon.

GROWS BEST FROM Seed, starts (look like a small green onion), or sets (look like a small onion).

HOW TO PLANT Plant seeds ½" deep and 1" apart. Transplant starts 1"–2" deep and about 1" apart. Plant onion sets (pointy end up) ½"–1" deep and 1"–2" apart.

LIGHT Full sun to partial shade.

WATER Water well until plant is established and then provide regular water. Onions grow well with an olla or in a self-watering container.

FEED Benefits from a liquid organic fertilizer application every other week during the growing season.

WHEN TO HARVEST Begin harvesting when stems are 5"–6" tall and the diameter of a pencil. Harvest all at once or harvest individual onions as needed.

Tips Mound up soil around the base of onions to block sunlight and encourage longer blanched (white) part of stem.

KALE

Cool-loving, leafy green that is easy to grow, good for you, and very happy in containers.

DAYS TO HARVEST 60–90

SIZE 10"–24" tall and wide, depending on variety

DIFFICULTY Level 1: Easy

Good to Know

Kale prefers cooler weather, and a light frost improves the flavor of kale. Warm weather often causes kale to bolt (go to seed). Good companions for kale include beets, cabbage, spinach, and Swiss chard.

How to Grow Kale

CONTAINER SIZE Extra-small (or larger, see "Container Sizes" in Chapter 2).

WHEN TO PLANT Begin planting 3–4 weeks before last spring frost date, and again in midsummer for a fall harvest. Plant kale in the fall and winter in hot summer areas. Succession-plant kale every 3 weeks throughout the growing season for a continual harvest of baby greens.

VARIETIES TO TRY Curly; Lacinato; Red Russian.

GROWS BEST FROM Seed or transplant. Look for small transplants.

HOW TO PLANT Plant seeds ½" deep and about 4" apart. Thin to 10"–15". Use thinned kale as baby greens. Plant kale transplants deeply up to the first leaves.

LIGHT Full sun to partial shade.

WATER Water well until plant is established and then provide regular water. Kale grows well with an olla or in a self-watering container.

FEED Benefits from a liquid organic fertilizer application once or twice during the growing season.

WHEN TO HARVEST Harvest individual leaves from the outside of the plant when they are about the size of your hand. The plant will continue to produce leaves from the inside out. Pick leaves when young; smaller leaves are milder-flavored and more tender than larger leaves.

Tips Aphids can be a problem. See Appendix A for organic pest control options.

Tips for Growing Indoors Ideal indoor temperature for kale is 70°F. Provide supplemental lighting. Set a timer to run the light for 14–16 hours with the light about 2"–4" away from the plant. Keep evenly moist.

KOHLRABI

Cool-loving, bulbous vegetable in the brassica family with a taste that resembles broccoli.

DAYS TO HARVEST 50–60 days (seed); 45–60 days (transplant)

SIZE 12"–18" tall and wide

DIFFICULTY Level 1: Easy

Good to Know

Kohlrabi prefers cool temperatures and doesn't mind a light frost. Kohlrabi needs even moisture for best flavor and texture. Good companions for kohlrabi include beets, broccoli, cauliflower, radishes, and onions.

How to Grow Kohlrabi

CONTAINER SIZE Small (or larger, see "Container Sizes" in Chapter 2).

WHEN TO PLANT Begin planting 3–4 weeks before the last spring frost. Plant kohlrabi in the fall in hot summer areas. Succession-plant kohlrabi every 2–3 weeks for a continual harvest.

VARIETIES TO TRY Quickstar (an early producer); Azur Star (a purple variety).

GROWS BEST FROM Seed or transplant. Select small transplants for the best chance of success.

HOW TO PLANT Plant seeds ¼" deep and 1" apart. Thin plants to 6" apart when seedlings are 2"–3" tall. Plant transplants at the same depth as nursery pots and space plants 6" apart.

LIGHT Full sun.

WATER Water well until plant is established and then provide regular water. Kohlrabi grows well with an olla or in a self-watering container.

FEED Benefits from a liquid organic fertilizer application once or twice during the growing season.

WHEN TO HARVEST For best flavor and texture, harvest kohlrabi when bulbs are 2" in diameter. Larger bulbs tend to be fibrous. To harvest, cut off just above ground level with a sharp knife.

Tips Aphids can be a problem. See Appendix A for organic pest control options.

LEMONGRASS

Large, heat-loving tropical plant with flat leaves grown for its lemon-scented thick stems and roots.

DAYS TO HARVEST 30–60 days from transplant

SIZE 2' tall and wide (or larger, depending on container size)

DIFFICULTY Level 1: Easy

Good to Know

Lemongrass stalks will multiply and should be divided every few years in warm-season climates. Lemongrass will quickly overtake its container and does best planted alone.

How to Grow Lemongrass

CONTAINER SIZE Medium (or larger, see "Container Sizes" in Chapter 2). Container should be 10" deep.

WHEN TO PLANT Begin planting after last spring frost.

VARIETIES TO TRY Normally one culinary variety.

GROWS BEST FROM Transplant.

HOW TO PLANT Plant transplants at the same depth as nursery pots and space plants 2' apart.

LIGHT Full sun.

WATER Water well until plant is established and then provide regular water. Lemongrass grows well in a self-watering container.

FEED Benefits from a liquid organic fertilizer application every other week during the growing season.

WHEN TO HARVEST Cut individual stalks as needed close to ground level. New stalks will form in their place. Don't harvest more than one-third of the plant at a time. Trim greens and peel away outer layers of plant to find the tender white heart used in cooking.

Tips Move indoors in cold climates to keep plant alive over the winter. Lemongrass prefers humid conditions. To increase humidity near plant, spritz the leaves with a water bottle.

LETTUCE

Cool-season group of crops grown for edible leaves with many varieties including leaf lettuce, romaine, head lettuce, and butterhead.

DAYS TO HARVEST 21–50

SIZE 6"–12" tall and wide

DIFFICULTY Level 1: Easy

Good to Know

Lettuce is an excellent choice for containers and often performs better there than in in-ground beds. Lettuce, especially leaf lettuce, is a fast grower. Hot weather or dry conditions cause lettuce to bolt and/or become bitter. Look for heat-resistant varieties when growing in warm climates. Good companions for lettuce include onions, radishes, and carrots.

How to Grow Lettuce

CONTAINER SIZE Extra-small (or larger, see "Container Sizes" in Chapter 2).

WHEN TO PLANT Begin planting 4 weeks before last spring frost date. Succession-plant every 2 weeks for a continual harvest. Plant lettuce again in the fall in warm climates.

VARIETIES TO TRY Sweetie Baby Romaine; Garden Babies Butterhead; Baby Mesclun.

GROWS BEST FROM Seed or transplant. Choose small transplants for best results. Transplants tend to bolt more quickly than lettuce planted from seeds.

HOW TO PLANT Spread seeds every ½" or so and lightly cover with soil. Do not let seeds dry out until they germinate. Thin seedlings and use as baby greens until leaf lettuces are about 4" apart and romaine and butterhead lettuces are 6"–8" apart. Plant transplants at the same depth as nursery pots; spacing depends on the variety.

LIGHT Full sun to partial shade.

WATER Water well until plant is established and then provide regular water. Lettuce has a shallow root system and needs frequent watering; do not allow lettuce to dry out. Water the soil, not the leaves. Lettuce grows well with an olla or in a self-watering container.

FEED Benefits from a liquid organic fertilizer application once or twice during the growing season.

WHEN TO HARVEST Harvest individual outer leaves as needed once plant is half-grown. To harvest entire plant, cut off with scissors ½" above the soil line.

Tips Lettuce does well when grown in a self-watering container with regular access to water.

MALABAR SPINACH

Heat-loving, fast-growing vine with large, succulent-like leaves grown as a hot summer alternative to spinach.

DAYS TO HARVEST 75

SIZE Vines quickly grow to 10' or longer in warm regions

DIFFICULTY Level 1: Easy

Good to Know

Malabar spinach is a fast grower and thrives in high temperatures but does not like to dry out. Raw Malabar spinach has a peppery, lemon flavor. Malabar spinach has a mucilaginous texture, somewhat similar to okra. Malabar spinach will quickly overtake any container it is grown in and is best planted alone.

How to Grow Malabar Spinach

CONTAINER SIZE Large (or larger, see "Container Sizes" in Chapter 2). Container should be at least 12" deep.

WHEN TO PLANT Begin planting after last spring frost and when the soil temperature reaches 65°F–85°F.

VARIETIES TO TRY Basella Rubra (has green leaves, light-pink flowers, and purple vines); Basella Alba (has green leaves, white flowers, and green vines).

GROWS BEST FROM Seed, transplant, or cutting.

HOW TO PLANT Plant seeds ¼" deep and 12" apart. Plant transplants at the same depth as nursery pots and space plants 12" apart. To grow from cuttings, trim the cutting to about 6" and plant directly in the desired area. Be sure to keep the area well watered to allow roots to form.

Cuttings can also be rooted in water and then planted.

LIGHT Full sun to partial shade; leaves are larger in partial shade. In full sun the leaves are smaller.

WATER Water well until plant is established and then provide regular water. Do not let dry out. Keep soil moist for best flavor. Malabar spinach grows well with an olla or in a self-watering container.

FEED Does not require supplemental feeding.

WHEN TO HARVEST Harvest leaves and shoots as desired once plant is large enough. Harvest new leaves for best flavor.

Tips Malabar spinach will quickly outgrow nearly any container. Keep it contained by trimming and harvesting frequently and providing a trellis for it to climb. Malabar spinach self-seeds easily; trim back vines once seeds develop and dig up unwanted seedlings.

MINT

Hardy perennial herb grown for its tasty leaves.

DAYS TO HARVEST 30 days after transplant, or once new growth appears and plant is 4"–6" tall

SIZE 6"–24" tall and about 18" wide

DIFFICULTY
Level 1: Easy

Good to Know

Mint is easy to grow. It is invasive and quickly spreads by underground stems that root and then form buds. Best grown by itself in a container or with other varieties of mint. Often dies back in cold-winter climates and then comes back in the spring.

How to Grow Mint

CONTAINER SIZE Extra-small (or larger, see "Container Sizes" in Chapter 2).

WHEN TO PLANT Begin planting after last spring frost date. Ideal soil temperature for planting is 55°F–70°F.

VARIETIES TO TRY Peppermint; Spearmint (lower growing and more compact); Apple; Chocolate.

GROWS BEST FROM Transplant. Smell leaves of transplants and buy one you like.

HOW TO PLANT Plant transplants at the same depth as nursery pots and space plants 12"–18" apart—if container is large enough. You can grow more than one variety of mint.

LIGHT Partial shade, especially in hot summer climates.

WATER Water well until plant is established and then provide regular water. Mint grows well with an olla or in a self-watering container.

FEED Benefits from a liquid organic fertilizer application at the beginning of the season.

WHEN TO HARVEST Harvest leaves often to encourage new growth. Never harvest more than one-third of the plant at a time.

Tips Keep flowers cut back to encourage growth. Divide plants every few years. If insides become woody, pull plant and replace.

Tips for Growing Indoors Ideal indoor temperature for mint is 65°F–70°F. Provide supplemental lighting. Set a timer to run the light for 12–13 hours and give the mint indirect light. Rotate plant each time you water to keep growth even. Keep evenly moist. Mist plant with water every few days to provide extra humidity.

NASTURTIUM

Trailing flower grown for edible leaves and blooms.

DAYS TO HARVEST 35–50 days to flower

SIZE 6"–3' tall and 12"–18" wide, depending on variety

DIFFICULTY Level 1: Easy

Good to Know

Nasturtium is frost-sensitive; keep covered if temperatures dip below 32°F. The flowers, leaves, and stems of nasturtiums are all edible. Good companion plant for tomatoes, radishes, and squash.

How to Grow Nasturtium

CONTAINER SIZE Extra-small (or larger, see "Container Sizes" in Chapter 2).

WHEN TO PLANT Begin planting after last spring frost. In mild winter climates, plant in the fall.

VARIETIES TO TRY Tom Thumb and Alaska Mix are both dwarf varieties good for containers.

GROWS BEST FROM Seed. Soak nasturtium seeds in a bowl of water for up to 8 hours before planting to speed germination.

HOW TO PLANT Plant seeds ½"–1" deep and 5"–6" apart. Keep seeds moist until they sprout.

LIGHT In cool climates, plant nasturtiums in full sun. In warm climates, grow plants in partial shade to prolong their growing season.

WATER Water well until plant is established and then let top inch of soil dry out a little between waterings.

FEED Nasturtiums do not need additional fertilizer. Supplemental feeding or soil that is too fertile results in fewer blooms and more leaves.

WHEN TO HARVEST Harvest leaves and flowers anytime after the plant begins to bloom. To harvest blooms and leaves for eating, pick early in the day (but after the dew dries).

Tips Keep nasturtiums trimmed back to keep plants tidy and to encourage blooming.

OKRA

Tall, warm-season vegetable with hibiscus-like flowers grown for its long pods.

DAYS TO HARVEST 50–65

SIZE 2'–3' tall and wide

DIFFICULTY
Level 1: Easy

Good to Know

Okra flowers and leaves are edible, both cooked and raw. Okra needs at least 60 days of very warm weather to grow well. In cooler climates, look for short-season varieties, or start seeds indoors. Good companions for okra include peppers and eggplant.

How to Grow Okra

CONTAINER SIZE Medium (or larger, see "Container Sizes" in Chapter 2). Container should be 10"–12" deep.

WHEN TO PLANT Begin planting okra 2 weeks after last spring frost date and at least 3 months before first fall frost date.

VARIETIES TO TRY Hill Country Red (shorter, fat pods with red tint); Baby Bubba Okra (smaller plant great for containers).

GROWS BEST FROM Seed.

HOW TO PLANT Plant seeds 3/4" deep and about 6" apart. Thin to 12" apart.

LIGHT Full sun.

WATER Water well until plant is established and then provide regular water. Okra grows well with an olla.

FEED Does not require supplemental feeding.

WHEN TO HARVEST Once okra flowers, it will be ready for harvest in 3–4 days. The taste of okra pods is best when they are harvested at 2"–3" long. Okra pods longer than 4" begin to be fibrous and inedible.

Tips Make it a point to harvest okra daily while it is producing; leaving pods on the plant slows or stops production. Always harvest okra by cutting with a knife or pruners; pulling the pods off can damage the plant.

OREGANO

Heat-loving, perennial herb with edible flowers and leaves. The savory, peppery leaves are often enjoyed in Greek and Italian dishes.

DAYS TO HARVEST 30 days after transplant, or once new growth appears and plant is 4"–6" tall

SIZE 12"–24" tall and 18" wide

DIFFICULTY Level 1: Easy

Good to Know

Oregano is a member of the mint family and can be invasive. Does best grown by itself in a container. Oregano thrives on neglect.

How to Grow Oregano

O

⬜ **CONTAINER SIZE** Extra-small (or larger, see "Container Sizes" in Chapter 2).

📆 **WHEN TO PLANT** Begin planting after last spring frost date. Ideal soil temperature for planting is 60°F–70°F.

🌿 **VARIETIES TO TRY** Greek (has a strong flavor); Marjoram (an herb similar to oregano, but the flavor is more mild).

🌱 **GROWS BEST FROM** Transplant. Smell leaves of transplants and buy one you like.

📥 **HOW TO PLANT** Plant transplant at the same depth as nursery pot.

☀ **LIGHT** Full sun; partial shade in very hot climates.

💧 **WATER** Water well until plant is established and then let top inch of soil dry out a little between waterings.

⚬ **FEED** Benefits from a liquid organic fertilizer application at the beginning of the season.

🌱 **WHEN TO HARVEST** Harvest leaves often to encourage new growth. Never harvest more than one third of the plant at a time.

Tips Keep flowers cut back to encourage growth. Divide plants every few years. If insides become woody, pull plant and replace. Bring indoors during the winter, or mulch containers well if you want to overwinter oregano outdoors. Keep plants healthy to avoid aphids and spider mites. Oregano does not like humidity.

Tips for Growing Indoors Ideal indoor temperature for oregano is 55°F–80°F. Provide supplemental lighting. Set a timer to run the light for 12 hours with the light about 2"–4" away from the plant. Rotate plant each time you water to keep growth even. Water only when top inch or so of soil is dry. Indoor-grown oregano does best in an unglazed terra cotta pot.

PARSLEY

Easy-to-grow biennial grown as an annual for its leaves. Favorite herb of cooks and enjoyed in Italian dishes.

DAYS TO HARVEST 30 days after transplant, or once new growth appears and plant is 4"–6" tall

SIZE 18"–24" tall (up to 3' tall when seed stalk forms) and 8"–12" wide

DIFFICULTY Level 1: Easy

Good to Know

Relative of carrot. Flowers in second year of growth and forms tall flower stalk that sets seed. Parsley is often grown as an annual and replanted each year for best flavor. Good companions for parsley include carrots and tomatoes.

How to Grow Parsley

CONTAINER SIZE Small (or larger, see "Container Sizes" in Chapter 2). Has a long taproot and does best in containers at least 8" deep.

WHEN TO PLANT Begin planting 5 weeks before last spring frost date.

VARIETIES TO TRY Giant of Italy (flat-leaved); Darki (curled parsley good for containers; only 12"–16" tall).

GROWS BEST FROM Transplant. Look for small, deep-green transplants; they will adjust better to planting. Seeds are very slow to germinate.

HOW TO PLANT Plant transplants at the same depth as nursery pots and space plants 6" apart.

LIGHT Full sun to partial shade.

WATER Water well until plant is established and then provide regular water. Parsley grows well with an olla or in a self-watering container.

FEED Benefits from a liquid organic fertilizer application once or twice during the growing season.

WHEN TO HARVEST Anytime; parsley is a quick grower. Harvest individual stalks as needed.

Tips Mulch in cool winter areas to overwinter. Rotate where you plant each year and clean up plant debris to prevent pests and disease.

Tips for Growing Indoors Ideal indoor temperature for parsley is 50°F–75°F. Set a timer to run the light for 10–11 hours with the light about 6" away from the plant. Water only when top inch or so of soil is dry. Indoor-grown parsley does best in an unglazed terra cotta pot.

PEAS

Cool-weather, early-spring vegetable that is easy to grow.

DAYS TO HARVEST 60–70

SIZE 2'–8' tall and 3"–6" wide, depending on variety

DIFFICULTY Level 1: Easy

Good to Know

Look for dwarf varieties that do better in containers. Provide a trellis for peas to climb. Good companions include carrots, turnips, and radishes. Do not plant onions or garlic near peas.

How to Grow Peas

CONTAINER SIZE Medium (or larger, see "Container Sizes" in Chapter 2).

WHEN TO PLANT Begin planting 5 weeks before last spring frost date.

VARIETIES TO TRY
- Shelling peas (inedible pod with full-size peas): Little Marvel.
- Sugar snap peas (edible pod with full-size peas): Little Crunch Container Snap Peas; Sugar Ann.
- Snow peas (edible pod with small peas): Oregon Sugar Pod II Snow Pea.

GROWS BEST FROM Seed.

HOW TO PLANT Put trellis in place and plant seeds 1" deep and 1"–2" apart on both sides of the trellis.

LIGHT Full sun to partial shade.

WATER Water well until plant is established and then provide regular water. Peas grow well with an olla or in a self-watering container.

FEED Benefits from a liquid organic fertilizer application once or twice during the growing season.

WHEN TO HARVEST Harvest peas when they are young, and harvest often. Leaving peas on the plant signals to the plant to slow or stop production. Harvest peas with two hands so vine is not damaged by pulling off peas. Harvest shelling and snap peas when peas are plump but not hard inside. Harvest snow peas when pods are flat and peas are not developed.

Tips If powdery mildew is an issue, select disease-resistant varieties, such as Oregon Sugar Pod II Snow Pea or Tendersweet Snap Pea seeds. Pea tendrils usually find the trellis; if they don't, guide them to the trellis and they should climb up it easily.

PEPPERS

Long-season, heat-loving bush plant in the nightshade family grown for its fruit that ranges from almost sweet to fiery hot.

DAYS TO HARVEST 60–100 days from transplant, depending on variety

SIZE 12"–24" tall and wide

DIFFICULTY Level 1: Easy

Good to Know

Peppers require warm weather to grow well. In cooler climates, peppers grow better in containers than in in-ground beds because the soil heats up faster. Pepper plants are brittle and do best with some staking or support to prevent branches from breaking. Peppers contain capsaicin, an oily compound that produces heat. The hotter the pepper, the more capsaicin the peppers contain. Use gloves when handling hot peppers; do not touch eyes or nose, as capsaicin can burn skin. Good companions for peppers include okra and eggplant.

How to Grow Peppers

CONTAINER SIZE Medium (or larger, see "Container Sizes" in Chapter 2). Container should be 8" deep.

WHEN TO PLANT Begin planting in the spring 2 weeks after last spring frost, once soil temperature reaches 70°F.

VARIETIES TO TRY Choose a sweet (e.g., Carmen or bell), medium (e.g., jalapeño), and hot pepper (e.g., habanero) for variety.

GROWS BEST FROM Transplant. Choose dense, compact plants and remove any blossoms before planting.

HOW TO PLANT Plant transplants at the same depth as nursery pots and space plants 12" apart.

LIGHT Full sun.

WATER Water well until plant is established and then provide regular water. Needs consistent moisture. Peppers grow well with an olla or in a self-watering container. Do not wet leaves; it may cause fungal disease.

FEED Benefits from a phosphorus-rich fertilizer at any stage of development.

WHEN TO HARVEST Pick peppers often to encourage production, especially early in the season. Fruit left on the plant signals to the plant to stop producing more fruit. Cut (don't pull) peppers off with pruners to prevent breaking branches. Leave 1" stem attached for longer storage life.

Tips Remove blossoms from plants for 1–2 weeks after planting to encourage good root development. Spray pepper plant with an Epsom salt solution (1 teaspoon Epsom salt to 32 ounces water) when blossoms appear to increase yield and boost overall health of plant.

POTATOES

Homegrown potatoes' taste and texture are a welcome addition to garden harvests, and, even better, potatoes happily grow in containers; no tilling required.

DAYS TO HARVEST 70–120

SIZE Depends on the size of container; plant will typically fill the container and grow 12"–24" above

DIFFICULTY Level 2: Medium

Good to Know

Potatoes grow well in acidic soil. For best results, look for a potting soil mix that supports acid-loving plants. Additionally, it's best to grow potatoes in their own container, not with any other plant.

How to Grow Potatoes

CONTAINER SIZE Medium (or larger, see "Container Sizes" in Chapter 2). Choose a container at least 18" wide and 2' deep.

WHEN TO PLANT Begin planting potatoes about 2 weeks after the last spring frost date, when soil temperatures are 45°F. In warm summer locations, potatoes are grown as a winter crop and can be started in late fall. Check your local planting guide for exact times.

VARIETIES TO TRY Early and new potatoes work best for planting in containers.

GROWS BEST FROM Pre-sprouted seed potatoes. "Chit" potatoes by letting "eyes" sprout in a cool, bright place indoors before planting. Cut large potatoes in half, but make sure there are at least two "eyes" on each potato. Let cut potatoes heal over for 1–2 days before planting.

HOW TO PLANT Important: Match the number of seed potatoes to the size of the container. Plant one seed potato per 2½ gallons of soil. Put 4" of soil in the bottom of the container. Place "chitted" potatoes sprout-side up 4" apart on soil. Cover potatoes with 4" of soil. (Easy to remember, right? 4-4-4). Once sprouted, plants are 6" high; cover all but the top leaves with more soil. Continue this process until the top of the container is reached.

LIGHT Full sun.

WATER Water well until plant is established and then provide regular water. Container should be kept evenly moist but not overly wet, or potatoes will rot.

FEED Benefits from a liquid organic fertilizer once or twice during the growing season.

WHEN TO HARVEST Plants will develop flowers and then the foliage will begin to die back. This is the best time to harvest. Harvest potatoes by dumping container out into a wheelbarrow.

Tips If you aren't sure if potatoes are ready to harvest, dig down and feel around. You should be able to find a potato or two and check the size. Potatoes are frost-sensitive and should be harvested before a frost.

RADISHES

Cool-season vegetable grown for its bulbous root. Comes in varying sizes and colors. Perfect crop for new gardeners.

DAYS TO HARVEST 25–60

SIZE 6"–12" tall and wide

DIFFICULTY Level 1: Easy

Good to Know

Radishes sprout easily, grow quickly, and are a perfect first vegetable to grow for first-time gardeners. Give radishes plenty of cool weather and moisture for milder flavor. Radishes grown in hot, dry conditions will be tough and spicy. Interplant radishes among slower-growing vegetables such as carrots and tomatoes. They will be ready to harvest before larger plants need the room. Good companions for radishes include beets, carrots, cucumbers, squash, and spinach.

How to Grow Radishes

CONTAINER SIZE Extra-small (or larger, see "Container Sizes" in Chapter 2).

WHEN TO PLANT Begin planting 3 weeks before last spring frost date. For fall planting, plant seeds up to 4 weeks before the first fall frost. Succession-plant radishes every week for a continual harvest.

VARIETIES TO TRY Easter Egg; French Breakfast; Watermelon Radish.

GROWS BEST FROM Seed.

HOW TO PLANT Plant seeds ½" deep and about 2" apart.

LIGHT Full sun to partial shade.

WATER Water well until plant is established and then provide regular water. Radishes grow well in a self-watering container.

FEED Benefits from a liquid organic fertilizer application once or twice during the growing season.

WHEN TO HARVEST Harvest radishes when small for best flavor. Radishes left in the ground quickly split or become fibrous and bitter.

Tips Trim greens from radishes after harvesting, as they take moisture away from the radishes.

ROSEMARY

Evergreen, heat-loving perennial grown for its fragrant, silvery, needle-like leaves.

DAYS TO HARVEST 60 days after transplant when new growth appears

SIZE 2'–3' tall and 2'–3' wide; size of container will limit size of rosemary

DIFFICULTY Level 1: Easy

Good to Know

Rosemary is native to the Mediterranean and is used to rugged, hot, dry conditions. Watering is the trickiest aspect of growing rosemary. Too much water and it will rot; too little and it will die. Using a clay or porous pot can help with airflow to the roots and prevent root rot. Good companions for rosemary include sage, broccoli, kale, kohlrabi, radishes, and thyme.

How to Grow Rosemary

CONTAINER SIZE Extra-small (or larger, see "Container Sizes" in Chapter 2).

WHEN TO PLANT Begin planting after last spring frost date. Ideal soil temperature for planting is 70°F–75°F.

VARIETIES TO TRY Tuscan Blue; Gorizia.

GROWS BEST FROM Transplant. Smell leaves of transplants and buy one you like. Seeds are very slow to germinate.

HOW TO PLANT Plant single transplant at the same depth as nursery pot.

LIGHT Full sun.

WATER Water well until plant is established and then let top inch of soil dry out a little between waterings. Good drainage is essential for rosemary. If you have a saucer underneath the pot, empty the saucer after watering.

FEED Benefits from a liquid organic fertilizer application at the beginning of the season.

WHEN TO HARVEST Harvest leaves often to encourage new growth. Never harvest more than one-third of the plant at a time. Best flavor is just before flowering. Keep flowers cut back to encourage production.

Tips Pinch tips back when small for a bushier plant. Bring inside during the winter in cold climates; will freeze in temperatures less than 25°F.

Tips for Growing Indoors Ideal indoor temperature for rosemary is 55°F–80°F. Provide supplemental lighting. Set a timer to run the light for 12 hours with the light about 5" away from the plant. Water only when top inch or so of soil is dry. Indoor-grown rosemary does best in an unglazed terra cotta pot.

SAGE

Hardy perennial herb grown for its fragrant, velvety leaves. Essential herb in stuffing and many savory dishes.

DAYS TO HARVEST 30–60 days after transplant when new growth appears

SIZE 12"–24" tall and wide

DIFFICULTY Level 1: Easy

Good to Know

This Mediterranean herb loves warm, dry conditions. Sage is grown as an annual in climates with high humidity. Each fall it sends up edible flowers. Sage does not tolerate hot, soggy soils; it will rot. Good companions for sage include rosemary, carrots, broccoli, kale, and kohlrabi. Do not plant sage near cucumbers or onions.

How to Grow Sage

CONTAINER SIZE Extra-small (or larger, see "Container Sizes" in Chapter 2).

WHEN TO PLANT Begin planting after last spring frost date. Ideal soil temperature for planting is 60°F.

VARIETIES TO TRY Holt's Mammoth (has large leaves); Tricolor (has purple, white, and green leaves). Try rubbing leaves between your fingers, smell, and then choose a variety you like.

GROWS BEST FROM Transplant. Smell leaves of transplants and buy one you like.

HOW TO PLANT Plant transplants at the same depth as nursery pots and space plants 24" apart.

LIGHT Full sun; partial shade in very hot climates.

WATER Water well until plant is established and then let top inch of soil dry out a little between waterings.

FEED Benefits from a liquid organic fertilizer application once or twice during the growing season.

WHEN TO HARVEST Harvest individual leaves the first year; harvest stems in subsequent years as needed.

Tips Prune back any woody stems each spring. Divide plants and replant every few years.

Tips for Growing Indoors Ideal indoor temperature for sage is 55°F–80°F. Provide supplemental lighting. Set a timer to run the light for 12 hours with the light about 5" away from the plant. Water only when top inch or so of soil is dry. Indoor-grown sage does best in an unglazed terra cotta pot.

SPINACH

Flavorful, frost-tolerant leafy green grown for its edible leaves.

DAYS TO HARVEST 30–50

SIZE 6"–12" tall and wide

DIFFICULTY Level 2: Medium

Good to Know

Spinach needs cool weather to grow well. It bolts quickly in hot or dry weather. Does best grown in early spring or fall. Look for both smooth-leaved and crinkly (savoy) types. Strawberries are an excellent companion plant for spinach.

How to Grow Spinach

CONTAINER SIZE Small (or larger, see "Container Sizes" in Chapter 2). Container should be at least 8" deep.

WHEN TO PLANT Begin planting up to 8 weeks before last frost and again in the fall. In mild winter areas, spinach can be grown all winter long.

VARIETIES TO TRY Bloomsdale (savoy type, slow to bolt); Auroch (smooth, fast-growing).

GROWS BEST FROM Seed; does not transplant well.

HOW TO PLANT Plant seeds ½" deep and 1" apart; thin to 3" apart to harvest as baby greens, 6" apart for full-size plants.

LIGHT Full sun to partial shade. In warm weather, providing shade will prolong production.

WATER Water well until plant is established and then provide regular water. Needs consistent moisture. Mulch soil to retain moisture. Spinach grows well with an olla or in a self-watering container.

FEED Benefits from a liquid organic fertilizer application every 2 weeks during the growing season.

WHEN TO HARVEST Harvest outer leaves at the base of the plant when leaves are 3"–4" long. Allow inner leaves to grow. Pick often to encourage growth. As temperatures climb, if flower buds form, the plant will bolt soon; harvest entire plant.

Tips Spinach tastes best when grown quickly with plenty of water and rich soil. Flat types are easier to clean than savoy types.

Tips for Growing Indoors Ideal indoor temperature for spinach is 40°F–75°F. Provide supplemental lighting. Set a timer to run the light for 12 hours with the light 2"–4" away from the plant. Keep evenly moist.

STRAWBERRIES

Low-growing, short-lived perennial grown for its sweet, bright red fruit.

DAYS TO HARVEST Up to 1 year after planting

SIZE 6"–12" tall and wide

DIFFICULTY Level 2: Medium

Good to Know

Containers are a good choice for growing strawberries to keep fruit up off the ground, away from pests. Strawberry leaves and blossoms grow out from the crown in the center of the plant. Strawberries are more difficult to grow in hot summer climates. There are different types of strawberries: day-neutral (smaller crop all season long, has fewer runners, good for containers); everbearing (larger crop in spring followed by smaller harvests later in the summer, okay for containers); and June-bearing (one larger crop in early summer, avoid for containers). Spinach is an excellent companion plant for strawberries.

How to Grow Strawberries

CONTAINER SIZE Small (or larger, see "Container Sizes" in Chapter 2). Container should be at least 8" deep. Look for self-watering strawberry plant containers.

WHEN TO PLANT Begin planting 4 weeks before last spring frost.

VARIETIES TO TRY Tribute; Tristar (day-neutral, good for containers); Quinault (everbearing with large, sweet fruit).

GROWS BEST FROM Transplants. Look for disease-resistant varieties that grow well in your area.

HOW TO PLANT Plant with crown (center) at soil surface. Do not cover the crown with soil; it can rot. Space plants 10" apart.

LIGHT Full sun; partial shade in very hot climates.

WATER Water well until plant is established and then provide regular water. Strawberries have shallow roots and need consistent moisture. Strawberries grow well with an olla or in a self-watering container. May need more water when fruits are developing. Mulch soil to retain moisture.

FEED Benefits from a liquid organic fertilizer application every 2 weeks during the growing season.

WHEN TO HARVEST Cut strawberries from plant (don't pull) when berries are bright red, shiny, and firm, leaving about ½" stem on berry. Harvest in the morning for best flavor. Once berries begin to darken and dull, they are overripe. Unripe berries will not ripen more once picked.

Tips Use netting or tulle to cover plants and protect from birds. Most strawberry plants produce runners (horizontal stems that produce new clone plants from the parent plant). It's best to cut off runners from plants to encourage the energy to go to the main plant rather than into producing runners. Replace plants every 3–4 years.

SUMMER SQUASH

Quick-growing, heat-loving fruiting vegetable whose fruits are harvested when young and tender.

DAYS TO HARVEST 45–60

SIZE 2"–3" tall and wide, depending on variety

DIFFICULTY Level 1: Easy

Good to Know

Most winter squash varieties are large vining plants and do not grow well in containers. Choose "bush" or "compact" types of summer squash for container gardening. Good companions include nasturtiums and radishes.

How to Grow Summer Squash

CONTAINER SIZE Medium (or larger, see "Container Sizes" in Chapter 2). Container should be at least 10" deep.

WHEN TO PLANT Squash needs warm soil to sprout and grow well. Begin planting in the spring after last spring frost. Seeds will germinate more quickly in soil temperatures above 70°F.

VARIETIES TO TRY Spacemaster; Eight Ball; Gold Rush; Patty Pan.

GROWS BEST FROM Seed.

HOW TO PLANT Plant two to three seeds 1" deep. Thin to strongest seedling when second set of leaves appears. Space plants 2' apart.

LIGHT Full sun.

WATER Water well until plant is established and then provide regular water. Needs consistent moisture. Summer squash grows well with an olla or in a self-watering container. Keep leaves dry to help prevent powdery mildew.

FEED Benefits from a phosphorus-rich fertilizer every 2–3 weeks during the growing season.

WHEN TO HARVEST Summer squash tastes best when small and tender. Harvest squash by cutting through the stem, not the main vine, with a sharp knife when fruits are 4"–6" long. The seeds will get larger and skin will become tougher as the fruit gets larger.

Tips Cover soil with garden fabric to warm the soil at the beginning of the season in cool climates. Plant cool-season crops like lettuce, radishes, and spinach in the container while you are waiting for soil to warm up in the spring. If you are finding that female fruits are withering and not getting pollinated by bees, try hand-pollination by transferring pollen from the male blossom (long, thin stem) to the female blossom (bulbous stem, looks like a small version of the fruit). Picking the fruit often encourages production.

SUNFLOWER

Iconic, sun-shaped annual flower that tolerates hot and dry conditions.

DAYS TO HARVEST 80–120 days, depending on the variety

SIZE 8"–2' tall and wide

DIFFICULTY Level 1: Easy

Good to Know

Many full-size sunflowers may be too large to be grown in containers. Choose dwarf and container varieties instead. Large seeds are easy to handle, germinate quickly, and are a great choice for gardening with children. Cucumbers are a good companion for sunflowers.

How to Grow Sunflowers

CONTAINER SIZE Small (or larger, see "Container Sizes" in Chapter 2). Container should be at least 12" deep.

WHEN TO PLANT Begin planting after last spring frost. In short-season climates, start seeds indoors 2–3 weeks before last frost.

VARIETIES TO TRY Teddy Bear; Kneehigh Sunflowers Music Box; Container Sunflowers Junior; Super Snack Mix (edible seeds).

GROWS BEST FROM Seed.

HOW TO PLANT Plant seeds about ½" deep. Keep moist until they germinate. Plant no more than one seed in an 8" container or three plants in a 12" container. In larger containers, space plants about 6" apart. Thin seedlings when they reach 3" tall.

LIGHT Full sun.

WATER Water well until plant is established and then provide regular water. Sunflowers grow well with an olla or in a self-watering container.

FEED Does not require supplemental feeding.

WHEN TO HARVEST Harvest edible buds when flower opens. Harvest petals by pulling them off once they open. Harvest seeds when they change from light to dark, the back of the flower fades from green to yellow and finally brown, and seeds are plump and firm.

Tips Succession-plant every 3 weeks for a continual harvest. Cover young seedlings with tulle to protect from birds.

SWEET POTATOES

Heat-loving, frost-sensitive vine grown for its bulbous, edible, nutritious root.

DAYS TO HARVEST 90–120

SIZE Vines grow quite large and will spill out of most containers

DIFFICULTY Level 2: Medium

Good to Know

Sweet potatoes grow well in very warm weather. You can grow your own sweet potato slips in about 2 months using a mature sweet potato. Bury bottom half of sweet potato in soil and keep warm and moist in bright light until shoots form. You can also suspend a sweet potato in water using toothpicks. Regardless of the method, remove shoots when they are several inches long, remove the leaves from the bottom half of the shoot, and put the bottom half in water. When shoots have several roots formed, they can be planted using the following directions. Sweet potatoes will quickly overtake their container and do best planted alone.

How to Grow Sweet Potatoes

CONTAINER SIZE Large (or larger, see "Container Sizes" in Chapter 2).

WHEN TO PLANT Begin planting sweet potatoes 2–3 weeks after the last spring frost, when the soil temperature is at least 65°F.

VARIETIES TO TRY Beauregard (short-season); Vardaman (compact vines, good flavor).

GROWS BEST FROM Slips (rooted sweet potato shoots grown from a mature sweet potato).

HOW TO PLANT Plant rooted slips 4" deep and 12"–18" apart.

LIGHT Full sun.

WATER Water well until plant is established and then provide regular water.

FEED About a month after planting sweet potatoes, fertilize with an organic fertilizer with phosphate and potassium to encourage root development.

WHEN TO HARVEST Harvest 90–120 days after planting, before the first fall frost, when the leaves and vines begin turning yellow. Dig down to check size of tubers; harvest when they are at least 3" in diameter. To harvest, cut back vines and loosen soil around the plant; carefully dig up the tubers. Handle tubers carefully to prevent bruising.

Tips For larger sweet potatoes, do not trim back vines; allow vines to spread and absorb sunlight. For longer storage, cure sweet potatoes after harvesting. To cure sweet potatoes, set potatoes in a single layer (not touching) in a warm (about 80°F), dark area for 10–14 days.

SWISS CHARD

Swiss chard is an easy-to-grow member of the beet family, grown for its colorful and nutritious stems and leaves.

DAYS TO HARVEST 50–90

SIZE 12"–18" tall and wide

DIFFICULTY Level 1: Easy

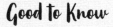
Good to Know

Swiss chard grows well in containers and doesn't mind a little frost or a little heat in the summer. It is very adaptable. Chard is relatively pest-free and easy to grow. Good companions include lettuce, radish, beans, broccoli, and thyme.

How to Grow Swiss Chard

CONTAINER SIZE Extra-small (or larger, see "Container Sizes" in Chapter 2).

WHEN TO PLANT Begin planting 2–3 weeks before last spring frost date.

VARIETIES TO TRY Bright Lights; Fordhook Giant; Barese (dwarf variety).

GROWS BEST FROM Seed or transplant. Look for small transplants for greatest chance of success.

HOW TO PLANT Plant seeds ½" deep and spaced 6"–8" apart. Each seed is actually a cluster of a few seeds. Once the seedlings are 3"–4" tall, thin them to one plant in each hole. Thin seedlings to 12" apart if desired for larger leaves. Plant transplants at the same depth as nursery pots and space plants 6"–8" apart.

LIGHT Full sun to partial shade.

WATER Water well until plant is established and then provide regular water.

FEED Benefits from a liquid organic fertilizer application once or twice during the growing season.

WHEN TO HARVEST Harvest when plants are 6"–8" tall. Harvest the outer leaves using the cut-and-come-again method.

Tips If chard's center stalk bolts (goes to seed), pull the plant, as the flavor will diminish.

THYME

Perennial herb grown for its small leaves that pack a delicious flavor.

DAYS TO HARVEST 30–60 days after transplant when new growth appears

SIZE 6"–8" tall and 10"–12" wide

DIFFICULTY Level 1: Easy

Good to Know

Thyme is easy to grow and very happy in containers. Thyme is a Mediterranean herb that tolerates hot, dry conditions. The flavor of dried thyme can't compare to growing it fresh yourself. Good companions include cabbage and nasturtiums.

How to Grow Thyme

CONTAINER SIZE Extra-small (or larger, see "Container Sizes" in Chapter 2).

WHEN TO PLANT Begin planting after last spring frost date. Ideal soil temperature for planting is 70°F.

VARIETIES TO TRY Creeping Thyme (low-growing thyme with purple blooms); Summer Thyme (has strong flavor).

GROWS BEST FROM Transplant. Smell leaves of transplants and buy one you like. Seeds are very slow to germinate.

HOW TO PLANT Plant transplants at the same depth as nursery pots.

LIGHT Full sun; partial shade in very hot climates.

WATER Water well until plant is established and then let top inch of soil dry out a little between waterings.

FEED Benefits from a half-strength dose of liquid organic fertilizer every 2 weeks during the growing season.

WHEN TO HARVEST Cut sparingly until established. Never harvest more than one-third of the plant at a time. Best flavor is just before flowering. Keep flowers cut back to encourage production.

Tips Mulch well in winter in cool climates. Cut back thyme each spring by half to encourage new growth. Thyme becomes woody and less aromatic after a few years and should be replaced.

Tips for Growing Indoors Ideal indoor temperature for thyme is 70°F. Provide supplemental lighting. Set a timer to run the light for 12 hours with the light about 2"–4" away from the plant. Rotate plant each time you water to keep growth even. Water only when top inch or so of soil is dry. Indoor-grown thyme does best in an unglazed terra cotta pot.

TOMATOES

Heat-loving member of the nightshade family grown for nearly endless varieties of edible fruit, and a favorite of vegetable gardeners because of the taste of homegrown tomatoes.

DAYS TO HARVEST 50–80 days from transplant

SIZE Bush varieties: 3' tall and wide; vining varieties: 6'–7' tall and 2' wide

DIFFICULTY Level 2: Medium

Good to Know

Tomatoes require a large amount of soil, water, air, and sunlight to grow well. Choose a sunny location and a large container, and give your tomatoes plenty of water. Tomatoes are divided into two types: determinate (grow a certain amount of fruit and size) and indeterminate (continue growing and producing fruit as long as conditions are right). Determinate types are a good choice for growing in containers. Choose disease-resistant, bush, and container varieties. Good companions for tomatoes include basil, carrots, onions, parsley, garlic, and nasturtiums.

How to Grow Tomatoes

CONTAINER SIZE Large (or larger, see "Container Sizes" in Chapter 2). Plant one plant in each container for best results. Overcrowding prevents good airflow. Ideally containers are 2' deep and wide.

WHEN TO PLANT Begin planting in the spring, after danger of frost has passed. Cover containers with garden fabric to warm soil in the spring. Warm-climate areas may also have a second planting window in late summer or early fall.

VARIETIES TO TRY Celebrity; Bush Early Girl; Roma; Gold Nugget; Tumbling Tom.

GROWS BEST FROM Transplant.

HOW TO PLANT Choose small, healthy-looking transplants with deep-green leaves. Remove bottom two-thirds of branches on plant. Dig a hole deep enough to plant tomato roots plus two-thirds of plant and stem. Roots will develop all along plant's stem underground. Add a trellis to the container at the time of planting so as not to disturb roots later on.

LIGHT Full sun.

WATER Provide steady, even watering. Do not let tomato plants or soil dry out. Tomatoes are an excellent choice for an olla or a self-watering container. Tomato plants often use up to a gallon of water each day. Problems such as cracking and blossom-end rot are often caused by uneven watering. Do not get water on leaves; this can cause problems with disease.

FEED Benefits from a liquid seaweed fertilizer application every 1–2 weeks during the growing season.

WHEN TO HARVEST Cover plants with netting or tulle to protect from birds. Color is the best indicator of ripeness. Harvest fruit by cutting stem.

Tips Provide support for growing tomatoes at time of planting; a tomato cage/trellis is a good way to support tomatoes. Pick off tomato hornworms and cutworms by hand. See Appendix A for organic pest control options. Once nighttime temperatures drop below 40°F cover plants or remove fruit.

TOOTHACHE PLANT

Heat-loving flower commonly called "toothache plant" for the tingly, numbing sensation after chewing the citrus-flavored leaves or gumdrop-shaped flowers. Formal name is Spilanthes.

DAYS TO HARVEST 60–90

SIZE 12" tall and 18" wide

DIFFICULTY Level 1: Easy

Good to Know

Toothache plant grows very well in containers and will often spill prettily over the sides. Does not tolerate frost; prefers very warm weather. The leaves, flowers, and buds are all edible. The highest concentration of the anesthetic effect is in the flowers.

How to Grow Toothache Plant

CONTAINER SIZE Extra-small (or larger, see "Container Sizes" in Chapter 2).

WHEN TO PLANT Begin planting after last spring frost, when the soil temperature reaches 65°F–85°F.

VARIETIES TO TRY Bullseye (red center); Lemon Drop.

GROWS BEST FROM Transplant (if you can find them) or seed.

HOW TO PLANT Plant transplants at the same depth as nursery pots and space plants 6"–12" apart. Sprinkle two to three seeds on top of soil every 6" and lightly water. Do not cover. Seeds need light and warm temperatures to germinate. Thin to 6"–12" apart when plants are 2"–3" tall.

LIGHT Full sun.

WATER Water well until plant is established and then provide regular water. Needs consistent moisture. Toothache plant grows well with an olla or in a self-watering container.

FEED Benefits from a liquid seaweed fertilizer application every 2 weeks during the growing season.

WHEN TO HARVEST Pick leaves once plant is established. Harvest flowers anytime. Keep flowers picked to encourage more blooms.

Tips Pinch back growing tips to promote fuller plants. Grown as a perennial in tropical climates; bring indoors for the winter if desired.

TURMERIC

Heat-loving, long-season tropical plant grown for its flavorful, deep orange rhizomes.

DAYS TO HARVEST 8–10 months

SIZE 3' tall and 2' wide

DIFFICULTY Level 2 or 3: Medium to Difficult, depending on climate; easier to grow in warm climates

Good to Know

Turmeric needs a long, warm growing season to grow well (zones 8 and above). In cooler climates (zones 7 and below), pre-sprout indoors (see following directions) 10 months before the first fall frost date, and then plant outside when the weather warms. Turmeric and ginger have similar growing requirements and can be near each other.

How to Grow Turmeric

CONTAINER SIZE Medium (or larger, see "Container Sizes" in Chapter 2). Container should be at least 10" deep.

WHEN TO PLANT Plant after last spring frost and the soil temperature reaches 55°F.

VARIETIES TO TRY Hawaiian Red is the variety typically sold in grocery stores.

GROWS BEST FROM Rhizomes. Using organic turmeric from the grocery store is fine. Cut large rhizomes into sections that each contain two or three buds. Let cut edges dry and heal over.

HOW TO PLANT Pre-sprout rhizomes in cool climates by planting a rhizome with two or three buds 2" deep in 3½" pots on heat mats. Keep warm and slightly moist (but not soggy; it will rot). Once turmeric sprouts, let it grow in a sunny spot until it is warm enough to plant outside. Let plants become accustomed to outdoor conditions for a week, and then carefully transplant to larger containers outdoors. In warmer areas plant rhizomes with buds pointing up 2"–3" deep and 6"–8" apart.

LIGHT Although turmeric needs warmth, it prefers partial shade, especially in warm-climate areas.

WATER Keep soil moist but not soggy until rhizomes sprout. Once turmeric is actively growing, water more frequently. Turmeric needs consistent moisture. Turmeric grows well in self-watering container. Mist plant occasionally in low-humidity areas.

FEED Benefits from a liquid seaweed fertilizer application every 2 weeks during the growing season.

WHEN TO HARVEST Harvest when leaves begin to yellow and die back, or before first fall frost. Harvest rhizomes by gently loosening soil and digging them up carefully. Cut turmeric stems off about an inch above the rhizomes after harvesting and rinse well.

Tips About once a month when turmeric is growing, add a 1"–2" layer of compost to container.

VIOLA

Flower family that includes violas, violets, pansies, and Johnny Jump-Up. These cool-loving annual flowers have heart-shaped leaves and multicolored edible blossoms.

DAYS TO HARVEST 60–70

SIZE 4"–12" tall and wide

DIFFICULTY Level 1: Easy

Good to Know

Violas are easy to tuck in around other plants and make good companions for most plants. They are often the first to bloom in the spring and will bloom again in late fall if they survive the heat of the summer. Hot weather causes viola blooms to fade and plants to die. Johnny Jump-Ups reseed easily year after year.

How to Grow Violas

CONTAINER SIZE Extra-small (or larger, see "Container Sizes" in Chapter 2).

WHEN TO PLANT Begin planting after last spring frost or in the fall for a second harvest.

VARIETIES TO TRY Johnny Jump-Up; Amber Kiss Viola (has a strong fragrance); Majestic Giant.

GROWS BEST FROM Seed or transplant. Look for small transplants; they will adjust better to planting.

HOW TO PLANT Scatter seeds on soil and cover with ¼" soil. Seeds take 7–14 days to germinate. Keep seeds moist until they sprout. Thin seedlings to about 8" apart. Plant transplants at the same depth as nursery pots and space plants about 8" apart.

LIGHT Partial shade.

WATER Water well until plant is established and then provide regular water. Violas grow well with an olla or in a self-watering container.

FEED Benefits from a half-strength application of liquid organic fertilizer every 2 weeks during the growing season.

WHEN TO HARVEST Pick blooms as needed.

Tips Deadhead blooms often to encourage fresh blooms. Cut back during the summer, and plant may bloom again in the fall.

APPENDIX A: TROUBLESHOOTING ADVICE AND A QUICK REFERENCE GUIDE FOR ORGANIC PEST CONTROL

The good news for container gardeners is that container-grown plants often have fewer problems with pests and disease than their in-ground counterparts. Using sterile potting mixes prevents soil-borne diseases that are difficult to treat. Issues with pests are often easier to spot in containers than in the ground. Early detection usually means the issues that do come up are easier to manage.

Avoid disease by choosing healthy plants and disease-resistant varieties. Healthy plants are the best defense against pests. Pests prefer plants that are weakened in some way. Water correctly and avoid getting water on leaves. Give plants enough room, and space plants properly for adequate airflow.

TROUBLESHOOTING ADVICE

PROBLEM	OFTEN CAUSED BY	SOLUTIONS TO TRY
Yellow leaves Slow growth Brown dry lower leaves	Underwatering	Increase watering. Use a moisture meter to get an accurate idea of moisture level.
Plant looks wilted and may have any or all of the following: • Wet soil • Brown leaves • Yellow falling leaves • New growth falling off • Floppy plant • Mold • Slimy or foul-smelling roots (root rot)	Overwatering	Stop watering until top inch or more of soil is dry. Remove flowers. Use a moisture meter to get an accurate idea of moisture level. Water only when soil is dry to the touch.
Blossom-end rot (a sunken spot on the bottom of fruit such as tomatoes, peppers, or eggplant that turns black and thickens)	Plant is unable to take up calcium from the soil due to uneven watering and fluctuations in soil moisture (not uncommon in first tomatoes of the season)	Keep soil evenly moist. Use self-watering containers or ollas. Mulch plants well.
Male and female blossoms are present, but female blossoms are withering and not forming fruit	Lack of pollinators	Pollinate plants by hand.

PROBLEM	OFTEN CAUSED BY	SOLUTIONS TO TRY
Slow growth	Not enough sun Lack of nutrients	Move the container to a location that receives more sunlight. Feed with an organic fertilizer.
Light-green or yellow leaves with green veining	Nitrogen deficiency	Feed with fish fertilizer.
Red or purple leaves	Phosphorus deficiency	Feed with seaweed fertilizer.
Powdery mildew, a white, powdery-looking substance on leaves; usually begins as small white spots on the top of leaves and spreads	Water on leaves Not enough sunlight or airflow Humid, wet conditions	Move container to sunnier location. Prune overcrowded branches or plants to increase air circulation. Spray plants with a solution of 1 teaspoon baking soda mixed with 1 quart water. Remove heavily infected plants.

QUICK REFERENCE GUIDE FOR ORGANIC PEST CONTROL

Observation is one of your best tools. Check plants daily, especially the undersides of leaves and the stem. If you see an adult pest, look for its eggs on undersides of leaves. If problems are spotted, check the following list and begin with the least invasive method. (In the table, the least invasive method is listed first.)

If a plant becomes overrun with pests, it may have reached the end of its life cycle. Pull and dispose of the plant rather than have the bugs spread to your other containers.

PEST	DESCRIPTION	TREATMENT	PREFERRED PLANTS
Aphids	Very small (under $\frac{1}{4}$") soft-bodied insect with pear-shaped body Usually found in large numbers Many different colors	Water spray Garlic spray Prune severely infected leaves and plants Insecticidal soap Neem oil	New growth on many plants
Cabbage worms/ loopers	Velvety green small ($1\frac{1}{4}$") larvae/caterpillar Eggs laid by white and yellow moths	Row covers Handpick Yellow sticky traps Bacillus thuringiensis (Bt) Garlic spray Neem oil	Broccoli, cabbage, cauliflower, kale
Flea beetles	Tiny ($\frac{1}{16}$") shiny black or brown beetle Jumps away when you get near	Row covers Yellow sticky traps Neem oil	Beans, broccoli, cabbage, eggplant, kale, lettuce, squash, tomatoes

PEST	DESCRIPTION	TREATMENT	PREFERRED PLANTS
Japanese beetles, Colorado potato beetles, cucumber beetles	Hard-shelled beetles, $\frac{1}{3}$"–$\frac{1}{2}$" long	Garden fabric Handpick adults and eggs Shake bugs off onto a drop cloth Neem oil	Beans, fruit trees, eggplant, potato, tomato, pepper, cucumber, squash
Pill bugs (roly-polys)—can be harmful to young plants when found in large numbers	$\frac{1}{2}$"-long black or brown crustacean with seven pairs of legs and a segmented body that rolls into a ball when disturbed	Good garden sanitation Handpick Beer, citrus, and board traps Diatomaceous earth Neem oil	Seedlings, young transplants
Slugs, snails	Slug: soft-bodied, slimy, 1"–2" long Snail: looks similar but with antennae and shell	Handpick (easiest at night) Beer, citrus, and board traps Diatomaceous earth	Seedlings, young transplants
Spider mites	Very tiny ($\frac{1}{50}$") yellow arachnid Infestation causes stippling or webbing of leaves	Spray off with a strong stream of water Garlic spray Insecticidal soap Neem oil	Leafy plants
Squash bugs	Eggs: brown and usually laid in groups on undersides of leaves Nymph: gray with black legs Adult: $\frac{1}{2}$" long with brown or gray body	Good garden sanitation Row covers Check undersides of leaves daily and pick eggs off leaves Handpick adults Garlic spray Insecticidal soap Neem oil	Squash, cucumber, cantaloupe, watermelon
Squash vine borers	Eggs: flat, brown, tiny, often found around base of squash Larva: up to 1"-long, white, fat body with brown head Moth: $\frac{1}{2}$" long, gray and orange with transparent green wings	Grow resistant varieties Garlic spray Row covers	Squash
Thrips	Tiny ($\frac{1}{50}$"–$\frac{1}{25}$") flying insect Looks like dark sliver on your plants	Water spray Yellow sticky traps Diatomaceous earth Garlic spray Insecticidal soap Neem oil	Onions, chive, fig

PEST	DESCRIPTION	TREATMENT	PREFERRED PLANTS
Tomato hornworm	Large (up to 5") green caterpillar with white and black stripes and large horn on one end	Row covers Handpick Bacillus thuringiensis (Bt) Neem oil	Tomato, eggplant, pepper, potato
Whiteflies	Small ($1/12$") white soft-bodied flying insect	Water spray Yellow sticky trap Garlic spray Insecticidal soap Neem oil	Tomato, eggplant, pepper, okra, sweet potato, cabbage, citrus trees

TREATMENT DESCRIPTIONS

Demonstrate patience and use any method with a light hand. All products, even organic ones, may unintentionally kill beneficial insects. Follow the dilution and application instructions exactly. Organic controls used incorrectly or in too high concentrations can be as dangerous as chemicals.

TREATMENT	DESCRIPTION
Bacillus thuringiensis (Bt) foliar spray	Biological control that causes death when ingested by caterpillars. Does not discriminate between pests and other caterpillars.
Beer, citrus	Place shallow containers filled with beer or citrus fruit cut in half facedown in the soil overnight to attract insects. Use board traps the same way. Collect and dispose of insects each morning.
Diatomaceous earth	Rough texture injures skin of soft-bodied insects. Apply 2" barriers around plants and reapply after rain. Be sure to purchase only organic, food-safe diatomaceous earth.
Garlic spray	Repels pests rather than killing them. Reapply after rain. Spray on leaves.
Insecticidal soap foliar spray	Damages cell membranes of soft-bodied pests. Apply early in the morning and then rinse off to prevent sunburn of leaves.
Neem oil foliar spray	Blocks progression of life cycle of pest and causes loss of appetite. May harm bees. Do not spray on flowers; use only where needed.
Row covers	Apply right after planting to prevent damage from pests while crops are young. Remove to allow for pollination.
Yellow sticky traps	Hang up near affected plants (do not lay on the dirt) to attract flying pests and disrupt their life cycle.

APPENDIX B: RESOURCES TO LEARN MORE ABOUT CONTAINER GARDENING

FURTHER READING

Gardening Under Lights: The Complete Guide for Indoor Growers. Halleck, Leslie F. (Portland, OR: Timber Press, 2018).

Container Gardening for Dummies. Marken, Bill, Suzanne DeJohn, The Editors of the National Gardening Association. (Hoboken, NJ: Wiley Publishing, 2010).

McGee & Stuckey's The Bountiful Container. McGee, Rose Marie Nichols, Maggie Stuckey. (New York: Workman Publishing, 2002).

The Vegetable Gardener's Container Bible: How to Grow a Bounty of Food in Pots, Tubs, and Other Containers. Smith, Edward C. (North Adams, MA: Storey Publishing, 2011).

Simple Steps to Success: Fruit and Vegetables in Pots. Whittingham, Jo. (New York: DK Publishing, 2012).

ONLINE RESOURCES

USDA Plant Hardiness Zone Map
https://planthardiness.ars.usda.gov/PHZMWeb
(Enter your zip code to find your plant hardiness zone.)

The Old Farmer's Almanac
www.almanac.com/gardening/frostdates
(Find the average date of the last spring frost and first fall frost for locations within the United States and Canada.)

Balcony Garden Web
https://balconygardenweb.com
(Website with an emphasis on growing in containers and small spaces.)

SUPPLIERS

Gardener's Supply Company
www.gardeners.com
(Excellent selections of containers, self-watering containers, grow bags, and gardening supplies.)

GrowOya
https://growoya.com
(Ollas for sale in different sizes.)

Johnny's Selected Seeds
www.johnnyseeds.com
(Seeds, including a selection of recommended container varieties, plants, and gardening supplies.)

Renee's Garden
www.reneesgarden.com
(Heirloom seeds, including many that grow well in containers.)

Botanical Interests
www.botanicalinterests.com
(Heirloom and organic seeds, including many that grow well in containers.)

Baker Creek Heirloom Seeds
www.rareseeds.com
(Heirloom seeds, books, and supplies.)

W. Atlee Burpee & Co.
www.burpee.com
(Seeds, gardening supplies, and containers.)

US/METRIC CONVERSION CHART

VOLUME CONVERSIONS	
US VOLUME MEASURE	**METRIC EQUIVALENT**
⅛ teaspoon	0.5 milliliter
¼ teaspoon	1 milliliter
½ teaspoon	2 milliliters
1 teaspoon	5 milliliters
½ tablespoon	7 milliliters
1 tablespoon (3 teaspoons)	15 milliliters
2 tablespoons (1 fluid ounce)	30 milliliters
¼ cup (4 tablespoons)	60 milliliters
⅓ cup	90 milliliters
½ cup (4 fluid ounces)	125 milliliters
⅔ cup	160 milliliters
¾ cup (6 fluid ounces)	180 milliliters
1 cup (16 tablespoons)	250 milliliters
1 pint (2 cups)	500 milliliters
1 quart (4 cups)	1 liter (about)

WEIGHT CONVERSIONS	
US WEIGHT MEASURE	**METRIC EQUIVALENT**
½ ounce	15 grams
1 ounce	30 grams
2 ounces	60 grams
3 ounces	85 grams
¼ pound (4 ounces)	115 grams
½ pound (8 ounces)	225 grams
¾ pound (12 ounces)	340 grams
1 pound (16 ounces)	454 grams

INDEX